The Roman Republic

The Roman Republic

Titles in the World History Series

The Roman Republic

Don Nardo

LUCENT BOOKS
An imprint of Thomson Gale, a part of The Thomson Corporation

THOMSON
™
GALE

Detroit • New York • San Francisco • San Diego • New Haven, Conn. • Waterville, Maine • London • Munich

For more information, contact
Lucent Books
27500 Drake Rd.
Farmington Hills, MI 48331-3535
Or you can visit our Internet site at http://www.gale.com

LIBRARY OF CONGRESS CATALOGING-IN-PUBLICATION DATA

Nardo, Don, 1947–
    The Roman Republic / by Don Nardo
        p. cm. — (The world history series)
    Includes bibliographical references and index.
    ISBN 1-59018-658-3 (hardcover : alk. paper)
    1. Rome—History—Republic, 510–30 B.C.—Juvenile literature. I. Title. II. Series.
DG231.7.N37 2005
937'.02—dc22
                                                                    2005015207

Printed in the United States of America

Contents

Foreword

Each year, on the first day of school, nearly every history teacher faces the task of explaining why his or her students should study history. Many reasons have been given. One is that lessons exist in the past from which contemporary society can benefit and learn. Another is that exploration of the past allows us to see the origins of our customs, ideas, and institutions. Concepts such as democracy, ethnic conflict, or even things as trivial as fashion or mores, have historical roots.

Reasons such as these impress few students, however. If anything, these explanations seem remote and dull to young minds. Yet history is anything but dull. And therein lies what is perhaps the most compelling reason for studying history: History is filled with great stories. The classic themes of literature and drama—love and sacrifice, hatred and revenge, injustice and betrayal, adversity and overcoming adversity—fill the pages of history books, feeding the imagination as well as any of the great works of fiction do.

The story of the Children's Crusade, for example, is one of the most tragic in history. In 1212 Crusader fever hit Europe. A call went out from the pope that all good Christians should journey to Jerusalem to drive out the hated Muslims and return the city to Christian control. Heeding the call, thousands of children made the journey. Parents bravely allowed many children to go, and entire communities were inspired by the faith of these small Crusaders. Unfortunately, many boarded ships captained by slave traders, who enthusiastically sold the children into slavery as soon as they arrived at their destination. Thousands died from disease, exposure, and starvation on the long march across Europe to the Mediterranean Sea. Others perished at sea.

Another story, from a modern and more familiar place, offers a soul-wrenching view of personal humiliation but also the ability to rise above it. Hatsuye Egami was one of 110,000 Japanese Americans sent to internment camps during World War II. "Since yesterday we Japanese have ceased to be human beings," he wrote in his diary. "We are numbers. We are no longer Egamis, but the number 23324. A tag with that number is on every trunk, suitcase and bag. Tags, also, on our breasts." Despite such dehumanizing treatment, most internees worked hard to control their bitterness. They created workable communities inside the camps and demonstrated again and again their loyalty as Americans.

These are but two of the many stories from history that can be found in the pages of the Lucent Books World History series. All World History titles rely on sound research and verifiable evidence, and all give students a clear sense of time, place, and chronology through maps and time-lines as well as text.

All titles include a wide range of authoritative perspectives that demonstrate the complexity of historical interpretation and sharpen the reader's critical thinking skills. Formally documented quotations and annotated bibliographies enable students to locate and evaluate sources, often instantaneously via the Internet, and serve as valuable tools for further research and debate.

Finally, Lucent's World History titles present rousing good stories, featuring vivid primary source quotations drawn from unique, sometimes obscure sources such as diaries, public records, and contemporary chronicles. In this way, the voices of participants and witnesses as well as important biographers and historians bring the study of history to life. As we are caught up in the lives of others, we are reminded that we too are characters in the ongoing human saga, and we are better prepared for our own roles.

Important Dates During the

ca. 1550–1069
Years of the New Kingdom in Egypt, in which a series of vigorous kings create an Egyptian empire.

753
Traditional founding date for the city of Rome by Romulus (as computed and accepted by Roman scholars some seven centuries later).

265
Having gained control of the Italian Greek cities, Rome is master of the whole Italian peninsula.

ca. 500–323
Greece's Classical Age, in which Greek arts, architecture, literature, and democratic reforms reach their height.

1600	1000	750	500	250

B.C.

ca. 1000
Latin tribesmen establish small villages on some of the seven hills marking the site of the future city of Rome.

ca. 563
Siddhartha Gautama, who will later be known as the Buddha, namesake of a major world religion, is born in northern India.

390
A force of invading Gauls defeats a Roman army at the Allia River.

264–241
Years of the First Punic War, in which Rome defeats the maritime empire of Carthage.

ca. 509
The leading Roman landowners throw out their last king and establish the Roman Republic.

Time of the Roman Republic

ca. 221
Chinese emperor Shih Huang Ti orders the construction of the Great Wall of China.

73–71
The escaped slave Spartacus leads the last of Rome's large slave rebellions but is eventually defeated by Marcus Crassus.

48
Caesar defeats Pompey in Greece, then travels to Egypt and takes Cleopatra's side in a local civil war.

31
Octavian defeats Antony and Egypt's Queen Cleopatra at Actium and gains firm control of the Mediterranean world.

225	100	50	0

218–201
Rome fights and defeats Carthage again in the Second Punic War.

58–51
Julius Caesar conquers the peoples of Transalpine Gaul.

27
The Senate confers on Octavian the title of Augustus, "the revered one," and he becomes, in effect, Rome's first emperor.

44
After declaring himself "dictator for life," Caesar is assassinated by a group of senators.

42
Mark Antony and Octavian (Caesar's adopted son) defeat the leaders of the conspiracy against Caesar at Philippi.

A Genius for the Practical

Throughout history, nations and peoples have displayed their own individual characteristics. They have evolved their own special ways of viewing the world around them and of dealing with that world. The ancient Greeks, for instance, were great originators and creators. They believed strongly in the worth of the individual and encouraged individual expression. They also loved beauty, which they saw everywhere in nature. The Greeks combined their creative energies with their love of beauty and produced magnificent original art, sculpture, architecture, literature, and philosophy. Part of the special genius that formed the basis of the Greeks' national character, therefore, was their creative spirit.

The Romans, on the other hand, produced few truly original cultural achievements. Especially in their early centuries, they had "little interest in philosophic speculation or in the search for beauty," the late classical scholar W.G. Hardy point-

ed out. This was partly because the Romans viewed the individual less as a free spirit and more as a part of something greater and more important—society itself. In Rome the individual was subordinate to the system, the Roman state, which operated under fair but rigid and conservative laws. The Romans, striving above all else to be good law-abiding citizens, emphasized self-discipline over self-expression. "The ideal Roman virtues," Hardy said, "were simplicity, seriousness, dignity, and piety . . . the proper performance of one's duty to the gods, to the state, and to one's family."[1]

Brilliant Imitators

Yet the Romans still managed to produce splendid cultural achievements, mainly because they were brilliant imitators. They regularly borrowed the most admirable aspects of the other civilizations they encountered. Speaking of his ancestors, the first-century-B.C. Roman historian Sallust admitted, "If they thought that anything an ally or enemy had was likely to suit them, they enthusiastically adopted it at Rome, for they would rather copy a good thing than be consumed with envy because they had not got it."[2] The Romans imitated Greek civilization more than any other. Over the course of many centuries, Rome adopted Greek ideas about the gods and religion, as well as Greek styles of sculpture, architecture, and literature.

The Romans, however, were not mere imitators. They had a profound ability to adapt the best ideas and inventions of others to their own needs with great efficiency. Often the Romans greatly improved on the ideas and inventions they borrowed. And nearly always they judged an idea's worth by its usefulness. Whereas the Greeks developed high culture to express their love of beauty, the Romans did so to meet the needs of society and the state. "Roman genius was called into action by the enormous practical needs of a world empire,"[3] wrote scholar Edith Hamilton. Indeed, Rome met these needs appropriately and impressively by producing a vast network of roads for the swift transport of armies and trade goods; miles of aqueducts, channels that supplied life-giving water to sustain hundreds of cities; and giant racetracks, arenas (like the Colosseum), and public baths, each of which accommodated thousands of people at a time. If, then, it is possible to describe the Roman national character in a single word, that word would be *practicality*.

Chapter One

Rome's Origins and Early Centuries

The story of the Romans, a remarkable people who built the greatest empire in the ancient world, begins in ancient Italy. The geography and climate of this boot-shaped peninsula, which extends some 500 miles (805km) southward from Europe into the Mediterranean Sea, were important factors in Rome's early development. In the north, the lofty, snow-covered Alps form a natural barrier separating Italy from the rest of Europe. While central Europe experiences harsh winters, Italy has a warm, pleasant climate most of the year. Several rivers, among them the Po, the Arno, and the Tiber, descend from the Apennines, the rugged mountains that stretch north to south through central Italy. On their way westward to the sea, these rivers pass through coastal plains and valleys covered in rich, productive soil. These warm, fertile regions of Italy attracted settlers from many parts of Europe and the Mediterranean. Among them were not only the ancestors of the Romans but also other groups that would profoundly influence Roman culture and history.

The Perfect Place to Build a City

Modern historians have proposed two principal theories about where the earliest Romans came from. In the first, the Romans originated in central Italy as part of the so-called Apennine culture (named after the mountain range). This society, which used tools and weapons made of bronze and practiced inhumation (burial of the dead), appeared circa 1800 B.C. About six hundred years later, the culture began to experience significant changes, including a transition to iron tools and weapons, population increases, and the replacement of inhumation with cremation (burning of the dead). It is possible that this change from a bronze-age to an iron-age society was due to cultural influences that steadily entered Italy from neighboring lands.

The second theory about the origins of the earliest Romans is that a group of Latin-speaking tribes migrated into Italy sometime in its Bronze Age. Some may have started in central Europe and come across the Alps in succeeding waves, one every two or three generations. Others may have originated farther east, traveled westward through what is now Serbia, and crossed the Adriatic Sea into eastern Italy. Then, slowly but steadily, they moved across the peninsula until one group arrived at and settled on the famous seven hills of Rome, along the Tiber River.

Archaeological evidence suggests that the earliest settlements on these hills appeared shortly before 1000 B.C. Their location had a number of natural advantages. First, it was surrounded by fertile plains. It was also at the center of trade routes moving west to east along the river and north to south along the western border of the Apennines. In short, wrote the first-century-B.C. Roman historian Livy, the

The well in the foreground and the simple stone huts beyond were typical of early Italian farms and villages, including those of the Romans.

Romulus Founds Rome

By the third or second century B.C., one version of Rome's founding had become the most widely accepted. This legend claimed that the Romans were descended from Aeneas, a prince of the ancient city of Troy, located on the western coast of Asia Minor. According to the story, when the Greeks sacked Troy about 1200 B.C., Aeneas escaped and sailed across the Mediterranean to the west coast of Italy. There he supposedly established a settlement near the Alban Mount, a steep hill about 15 miles (24km) south of the Tiber. Among Aeneas's descendants were twin boys named Romulus and Remus. A cruel king condemned the infant boys to be left outside to die. But a mother wolf found the babies and nursed them. Then a shepherd took the boys in and raised them. When Romulus and Remus reached adulthood, they decided to establish a city on the Tiber but fought over the exact location. During the argument, Romulus slew his brother. And in this way, Romulus ended up establishing the city alone and became its first king.

In this Renaissance painting, a mother wolf nurses the infants Romulus and Remus. According to legend, Romulus eventually founded Rome.

site on which Rome grew was a strategic location for a city:

> Not without reason did gods and men choose this spot for the site of our city—the [life-giving] hills; the river to bring us produce from the inland regions and sea-borne commerce from abroad; the sea itself, near enough for convenience yet not so near as to bring danger from foreign fleets; [and] our situation in the very heart of Italy. All these advantages make it of all places in the world the best for a city destined to grow great. [4]

The first crude settlements in the area appeared on the three most prominent of the seven Roman hills—the Capitoline, the Palatine, and the Aventine. The exact dates and circumstances surrounding the origins of these settlements remain unclear. Later Romans accepted the date of 753 B.C. for the city's founding. But the Romans did not begin keeping regular historical records until the third century B.C. By that time the events of Rome's earliest years had become confused and shrouded in legend. It is more likely that the traditional founding date was based on faded recollections of the time when the scattered settlements on the hills merged into a single town—Rome.

Another part of the official legend was that Rome was first established by two young men named Romulus and Remus. Supposedly they were descended from Aeneas, a prince of the city of Troy (in Asia Minor, what is now Turkey). There is no proof that these persons ever existed. But it is possible that Romulus was an important early Roman leader whom later generations remembered fondly.

The Importance of Family and Religion

However their city was established, the Latins who first settled the Roman hills had a relatively primitive culture. They lived in simple huts with walls made of dried mud and roofs made of thatch (bundled twigs and plant stalks). They could not read or write, produced no arts, and had no strong central government.

In these early days, as remained true throughout the rest of Roman history, the family (*familia*) was the most important social unit. The male heads of families (patresfamilias) commanded the most power and respect in the community. Because the paterfamilias of each family controlled all aspects of the lives of his wife, children, and servants, Roman society was completely dominated by adult males. Women and children, as in most other ancient societies, had no rights and were not allowed to make important decisions for themselves.

Still, most Roman family heads were not petty tyrants. Cases of fathers throwing their wives or children out or killing them were rare. And over time new laws set various restrictions on the powers of a paterfamilias. Also, calls from a father's relatives, friends, or peers for him to act reasonably tended to restrain him from unusually cruel behavior. According to scholar Harold Johnston, "Custom, not law, obliged the paterfamilias to call a council of relatives and friends when he contemplated inflicting severe punishment upon his children, and public opinion obliged him to abide by its verdict."[5]

Just as the traditional, rigid family structure exerted a powerful influence over the lives of the early Romans, so did religion. Like other Latin tribes, the Romans worshipped spirits that they believed resided in everything around them, including inanimate objects such as rocks and trees. This kind of belief system is known as animism. At first the Romans pictured these spirits, called *numina,* as natural powers and forces rather than as thinking deities, or gods. In time, however, some of the spirits began to take on humanlike personalities. These became gods and goddesses, such as Vesta, goddess of the hearth, and Mars, who watched over farmers' fields.

Etruscan Influences

Roman religion, along with numerous other aspects of Roman life, was highly influenced by the cultures of other peoples. Most influential of all were the Etruscans and Greeks. The Etruscans were an energetic, talented, highly civilized people who lived in well-fortified cities, most of them located in the region directly north of Rome. The area was then known as Etruria, and today as Tuscany. (Both names derive from the name of the people.)

Because the Etruscans were more culturally advanced than the Romans, the latter borrowed a number of customs and concepts from their northern neighbors. The Etruscans constructed many stone buildings, bridges, and sewer drains. So they were able to teach the Romans much about stonemasonry and other building techniques, including the use of the curved arch that eventually became a Roman trademark.

The Romans also adopted some of the Etruscan gods. Among the most important were Jupiter (the Roman version of the Etruscan Tinia), god of the sky; Juno (from the Etruscan Uni), patron goddess of women; and Minerva (from the Etruscan Menerva), the goddess who protected craftspeople.

The Roman Monarchy

In addition, the Etruscans may have introduced some political ideas to the Romans. Etruscan towns were ruled by individual kings who held absolute power over their people. The early Romans, too, developed a system of rule by kings. If the first Roman king was really named Romulus, as the legend claims, he was probably the strongest local paterfamilias of the day, rather than the city's founder. The later Romans remembered six other kings following Romulus: Numa Pompilius, Tullus Hostilius, Ancus Marcius, Tarquinius Priscus, Servius Tullius, and Tarquinius Superbus (or "Tarquin the Proud"). Some of these men were likely real, but others, say modern scholars, were probably legendary. In fact, from a historical standpoint the actual length of and number of rulers in the period of kings—the Roman Monarchy—remain unclear.

Also uncertain is the manner in which the Roman kings were chosen, the exact nature of their duties, and the extent of their authority. Livy and other later writers mention a sort of election in which some of the male citizens took part. The right to vote

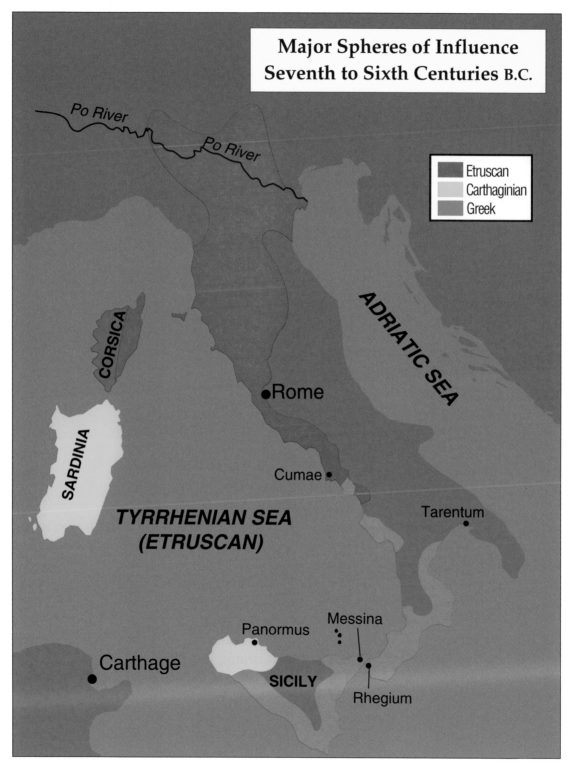

Major Spheres of Influence Seventh to Sixth Centuries B.C.

Po River

Po River

Legend:
- Etruscan
- Carthaginian
- Greek

ADRIATIC SEA

CORSICA

SARDINIA

Rome

TYRRHENIAN SEA (ETRUSCAN)

Cumae

Tarentum

Messina

Panormus

Carthage

SICILY

Rhegium

The Roman kings were advised by a board of well-to-do, respected elders called senators, seen here in session.

was probably based on certain property qualifications, including ownership of armor and weapons, which were quite expensive at the time. So, as happened in Greece during the same period, the community's fighting men met in an assembly, a periodic meeting to consider vital political and social policies. The real power seems to have been in the hands of the king and to a lesser extent his advisory board, the Senate, which would later become a true legislature with much authority. Nevertheless, the men who met in the assembly likely ratified the choice of monarch, as well as his major policies.

Greater Greece

The Romans also felt the influence of the Greeks. This happened partly indirectly, through the Etruscans, who were themselves strongly affected by Greek influences. Over time, the early Romans also had some direct contact with Greek cities in Italy. In the 700s B.C. powerful Greek cities such as Athens, Corinth, and Miletus began establishing colonies around the Mediterranean. The Greeks built cities along the coasts of Sicily, the large island lying at the foot of the Italian boot, the most prosperous of these being Syracuse. They also settled in southern and

The Early Romans Erect a Temple

Partly in imitation of Etruscan cities such as Veii (about 10 miles [16 km] north of Rome), in the late sixth century B.C. Rome began its transformation from a crude, ramshackle town to one with stone sewers, a paved forum (main square), and some stone public buildings. The most imposing of these early structures was the first of Rome's temples to its chief god, Jupiter. According to Livy's history (excerpted in The Early History of Rome), *its construction was supervised by Rome's last king, Tarquin the Proud:*

The project involved the use not only of public funds but also of a large number of laborers from the poorer classes. The work was hard in itself, and came in addition to their regular military duties; but it was an honorable burden with a solemn religious significance, and they were not, on the whole, unwilling to bear it.

A late Renaissance painting shows Romans gathering for the inauguration of the Temple of Jupiter in the sixth century B.C.

western Italy. After a century of colonization, there were so many Greek towns in southern Italy that the Latins began calling the region Magna Graecia, or "Greater Greece."

The Greeks were even more culturally advanced than the Etruscans, so it is not surprising that Greek customs and ideas affected Rome so profoundly. Greek traders introduced systems of coinage and weights and measures to the Romans. The Greeks also introduced their alphabet, much of which they had borrowed from the Phoenicians, a Near Eastern people known for their intensive commercial activities. This enabled the Romans to begin writing down their language.

In addition, Greek religious concepts influenced those of the Romans. The Greeks had an elaborate collection of gods, many of whom the Romans came to see as counterparts of their own. For example, the Romans equated the powerful Greek god Zeus, who ruled the heavens, with their own sky god Jupiter. And Zeus's wife Hera, queen of the Greek gods, was associated with the Roman goddess Juno. Inspired by the Greeks, the Romans enhanced the images of some existing gods. In this way, Mars, associated with the Greek war god Ares, became the Roman patron of warriors as well as protector of the fields. The Greek god Poseidon, lord of the seas, became the Roman god Neptune; Aphrodite, the Greek goddess of love, became the Roman Venus; and the Greek Artemis, goddess of animals and the hunt, became the Roman Diana. The Romans also adopted some new gods from the Greeks, such as Apollo, god of prophecy, healing, the sun, and music.

Maintaining Old-Fashioned Values

During the period of the Monarchy, the Romans continued to view the Etruscans and Greeks as superior cultures to be imitated rather than as economic and military rivals. This was because Rome was still a small farming community that controlled only a tiny portion of western Italy. The Romans had no trading fleets of their own, so they could not compete effectively with the more powerful and prosperous peoples to the north and south. The lucrative trade routes and markets of the western Mediterranean were dominated by the Etruscans, the Greeks, and the Phoenicians.

While these peoples controlled the big trade routes, the Romans remained content with working their farms and maintaining their traditional lifestyles. For centuries they had lived simple, practical lives built around family and community, with few frills and luxuries. Although they acquired many new products and ideas from the Etruscans, Greeks, and others, the Romans preferred to maintain their old ways as much as possible. In fact, mostly they adopted only those outside ideas and inventions that made their lives more efficient and their homes and families more secure. During these centuries the Romans strengthened the conservative values they most admired in themselves and in others. These included duty to family and community, respect for the gods, contempt for luxury and immorality, and a serious, dignified attitude toward self and life.

Even as Roman values remained the same, by the end of the sixth century B.C.

The Phoenicians in Italy

The Phoenicians were a prosperous maritime people based along the coasts of Palestine, in the eastern Mediterranean. In the late 800s B.C. they founded the city of Carthage in North Africa, and went on to establish trading posts in Spain, in southern Gaul (what is now France), and on the islands of Sardinia and Sicily. The latter excursions brought them into close proximity with the western Italian coasts. A vigorous trade ensued, in which the early Etruscans received Spanish gold and other valuables in exchange for their own copper and tin. The Phoenicians also set up small trading posts at Etruscan ports, including Punicum, the port town of Tarquinii, and Pyrgi, the port of Caere. Through the Etruscans, Phoenician cultural and commercial influences eventually reached Rome.

These once elegant mosaics were created by Phoenicians who lived and worked on a small island off the coast of Sicily.

A nineteenth-century engraving depicts the Roman people celebrating the expulsion of the king and establishment of the Republic.

Roman political ideas began to undergo a dramatic change. The city had grown increasingly prosperous and some patresfamilias had become as rich as the kings. This social class of wealthy landowners—the patricians—demanded a greater say in government. During this same period a number of Greek cities threw out their kings and instituted governments run by councils of local leaders. Such revolutionary political concepts inspired the Romans, especially the patricians. About the year 509 B.C., the Romans rid themselves of their king and established a republic, a government administered by popularly elected officials. Rome's spectacular rise from a backward village on the Tiber to master of its world had begun.

Chapter Two

Foundation and Expansion of the Republic

When the Romans set up the Republic in the late sixth century B.C., Rome was a small city-state that controlled only a tiny section of Italy. The city and its surrounding villages and farms covered perhaps 600 square miles (966km), about the size of New York City. The total population of Roman territory at the time, including slaves, was perhaps 260,000.

In addition, the Romans were hemmed in on all sides by other peoples. North of the Tiber stretched Etruria, still controlled by the powerful Etruscans. And directly south and east of Rome other Latin tribes held sway. Farther east in the Apennine foothills lived several fierce mountain tribes, including the Sabines, Umbrians, Volsci, and Aequi. Meanwhile, another Italian tribe, the warlike Samnites, controlled part of western Italy, and the Greeks dominated Italy's southern coastal regions.

With Rome being surrounded by so many foes, the odds of its very survival, much less its successful expansion, seemed small. Yet in a little more than two centuries, Rome defeated all of these peoples and took possession of all Italy. The Romans accomplished this formidable feat mainly because they were highly organized and efficient, both militarily and politically. The Roman Republic evolved by degrees into a strong, flexible government that answered the needs of most of its people. This instilled profound feelings of pride and patriotism in the Roman people. They came to believe not only that their system was superior to those of their neighbors but that Rome's expansion and conquests were fated by the gods. The combination of Roman efficiency and the belief that the Romans were divinely destined to conquer and rule others made Rome an unstoppable force in the early years of the Republic.

Giving the People a Voice

Two major factors led to the overthrow of Rome's kings and the establishment of the Republic. First, some of these rulers were corrupt. The last Roman king, Tarquin the Proud, for instance, had seized the throne after murdering the former king. He then arrested several leading patricians on false charges so that he could seize their wealthy estates for himself.

The second factor was economic. Since the seventh century B.C., a group of the most respected patricians had met periodically to advise the kings and discuss the problems of the community. Because they were also known as elders, or *senatores*, this group was called the Senate. At first, the senators had no real political power. As some Roman farms grew large and successful in the sixth century B.C., however, the patricians who owned them became increasingly wealthy and powerful. Eventually, these men became strong and bold enough to take complete control of the state. In about 509 B.C., after Tarquin's son raped the daughter of a prominent patrician, the Senate met, declared Tarquin's rule null and void, and created a new government.

The noted censor Claudius Appius (center, with the white beard) is escorted into a meeting of the Senate, Rome's most important legislature.

In setting up the Republic, the Romans wanted to create a system in which the people had a voice. By "the people," however, they did not mean average Romans of minimal means, who made up the vast majority of the population. Instead, they meant free men who owned at least some property. Included were the aristocratic, wealthy patricians and the few commoners who had enough money to own well-made weapons, which were very expensive at the time. These individuals were allowed to meet periodically in an assembly to discuss and vote on important issues and elect leaders.

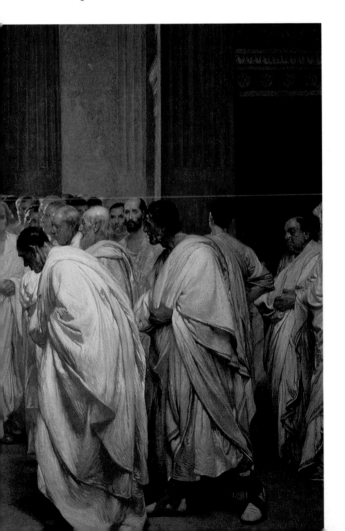

Excluded from the system were poor people, women, and slaves. Still, for its time, the idea of a government run by even a small portion of the populace, as opposed to a king, was both revolutionary and enlightened.

The men who met in the assembly elected two governing officials called consuls. These two men, who served jointly for a year, administered state affairs and led the army in wartime. There was also a provision for appointing a dictator. In a national emergency, he would run the country for a term of six months and then step down. Meanwhile, the Senate remained as an advisory body to aid the consuls in making decisions. The senators, all well-to-do patricians, served for life.

It soon became clear that the affairs of state were too complex for the consuls to manage alone. So each year the assembly elected various other officials to help run the government. Eventually these included eight praetors, or court judges; four aediles to manage the streets and public buildings; two censors, responsible for census taking, enrolling new senators, and inspecting morals and conduct; and twenty financial administrators called quaestors.

Gaining Veto Power

The new Roman government was not a true democracy like the ones in Athens and some other Greek cities, because only a privileged few took part in government. Since Roman public officials were not paid, only the well-to-do could afford to serve regularly. Also, some political offices were closed to common people,

A Roman Describes the Chief Magistrates

In his Laws *(quoted here from Niall Rudd's translation), the great first-century-B.C. Roman orator Cicero described the republican offices of consul and dictator, the latter to be filled in a national emergency.*

There shall be two [magistrates] with royal power. . . . They shall be called consuls. They shall hold the supreme military power and shall take orders from no one. To them, the safety of the people shall be the highest law. . . . But when a particularly serious war or civil disorder occurs, one man shall for a period no longer than six months hold power equal to that of the two consuls, if the Senate so decide. After being appointed under favorable auspices [omens], he shall be master of the people. He shall have an officer [known as the Master of the Horse] to command the cavalry.

called plebeians (or plebs for short). In addition to patrician domination of the Senate, only patricians could become consuls. And the patricians controlled the assembly through a system known as patronage, in which poor plebs (the clients) received financial or legal aid from wealthy patricians (the patrons). In exchange for this help, the clients voted in the assembly as instructed by their patrons.

Many plebs resented being excluded from the political process. Almost immediately after the creation of the Republic, they began demanding more say in government. At first the patricians ignored their demands, but soon the plebs went on strike, refusing to serve in the military. Without plebeian soldiers, the consuls could not raise the armies they needed to defend the city. "In Rome there was something like a panic," Livy recalled.

Everything came to a standstill. The commons [plebs] feared violence at the hands of the senatorial party, who, in their turn, were afraid of the commons. . . . How long would the deserters remain inactive? What would happen if . . . there was a threat of foreign invasion? Clearly the only hope lay in finding a solution for the conflicting interests of the two classes in the state.[6]

Seeing no other choice, the patricians gave in. In 494 B.C. they allowed the plebs to set up a separate popular assembly that excluded patricians. Although this assembly lacked the power to make laws, each year it elected ten plebeian officials called tribunes to look after the commoners' interests. The tribunes had the power to say *"Veto!"* ("I forbid!") and stop the passage of any laws proposed by the patricians.

A System Based on Law

Over time, the plebs won other political concessions from the patricians. One of these concerned the law. Corrupt patrician judges often misquoted or altered the laws, which were still unwritten, in order to convict accused plebs. In about 450 B.C. the plebs ended this corruption by demanding that Rome's laws be written down. The result was the Twelve Tables, a list of rules that became the basis of Rome's fair and efficient legal system.

More political reforms were enacted in the years that followed. In 366 B.C., for example, the consulship was opened to plebs, and it soon became customary to elect one patrician and one plebeian consul each year. Finally, in 287 B.C. the Popular Assembly gained the power to make laws.

The system was still far from ideal, however. Most plebs could not afford to quit their jobs to serve the state, and many continued to vote as instructed by wealthy

A crowd gathers to witness the posting of the Twelve Tables. These tablets, now lost, contained Rome's first codified laws.

Early Roman soldiers prepare for battle. These militiamen were all property owners who fought during an emergency and then returned to their farms.

patrician senators. Because the senators profoundly influenced the domestic and foreign policies of the consuls, Rome's real power still lay in the elite Senate. Nevertheless, Roman citizens—even poor ones—still had some voice in government. And most Romans viewed their system with pride. Indeed, a majority of Romans were extremely patriotic and willing to risk their lives to defend the state.

Early Roman Expansion

Such patriotism was certainly needed, for in its early centuries the Republic fought many wars against its neighbors. The first important military campaign was against the other Latin tribes, who opposed Roman expansion. In a great battle fought in 496 B.C. at Lake Regillus, about 15 miles (24km) southeast of Rome, the Romans fought and defeated a large army of Latins. Shortly afterward Rome signed a treaty with the Latins, which stated in part:

Let there be peace between the Romans and all the Latin cities as long as heaven and earth shall stay in the same position. Let them neither

A New, Flexible Army

After their defeat by the Gauls in 390 B.C., the Romans overhauled their army. Under the new system it no longer consisted simply of a big mass of soldiers but broke down into several smaller units on the battlefield. These units were called maniples (in Latin *manipuli,* which means "handfuls"). Each maniple could act independently of the others and also could combine with them in various ways, which made the army as a whole much more flexible. Each soldier now carried an oval-shaped (later rectangular) shield called the *scutum,* which afforded him excellent protection. He also carried one or two throwing spears, or *pila,* and a sharp thrusting sword, the *gladius.* Because the new Roman military system emphasized maniples as basic tactical units, it became known as the manipular system.

Once this new army was fully developed, its superior offensive and defensive features virtually ensured the success of future Roman conquests and expansion. The system's strongest points were its flexible organization, which exploited the strengths of various kinds of fighters; the excellent, often precision training and drilling given these fighters; and the strategic thought given to the many possible situations that might arise in battle, including the need for an ordered retreat.

Rome's manipular army featured different kinds of fighters, each employing unique weapons and tactics.

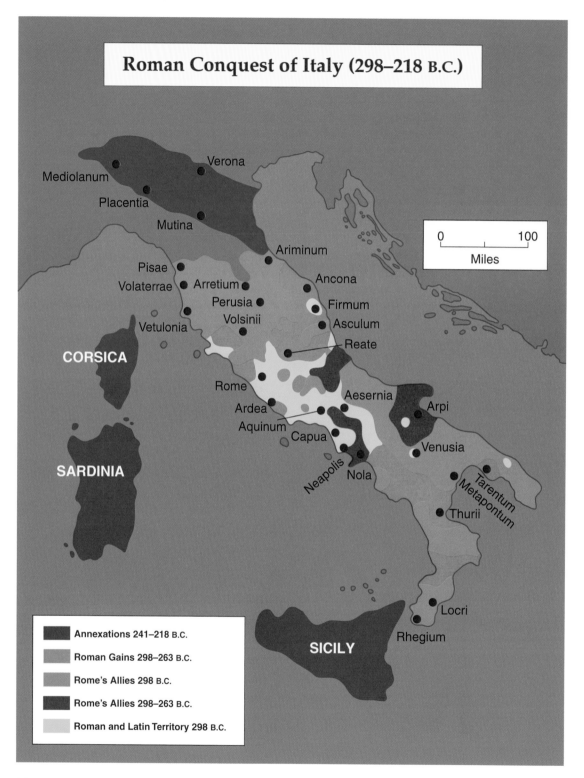

Roman Conquest of Italy (298–218 B.C.)

Mediolanum

Verona

Placentia

Mutina

Ariminum

Pisae

Arretium

Ancona

Volaterrae

Perusia

Firmum

Volsinii

Asculum

Vetulonia

Reate

CORSICA

Rome

Aesernia

Ardea

Arpi

Aquinum

Capua

Venusia

Neapolis

Nola

SARDINIA

Tarentum
Metapontum

Thurii

Locri

SICILY

Rhegium

0   100
Miles

Annexations 241–218 B.C.

Roman Gains 298–263 B.C.

Rome's Allies 298 B.C.

Rome's Allies 298–263 B.C.

Roman and Latin Territory 298 B.C.

make war upon one another . . . nor call in foreign enemies . . . but let them assist one another with all their might . . . and let each have an equal share of the spoils and booty taken in their common wars.[7]

Such lenient treatment of defeated peoples became a Roman tradition. Instead of imposing harsh, dictatorial rule on conquered enemies, the Romans drew up alliances with them and granted them either full Roman citizenship or a list of guaranteed rights. The Romans built roads and public buildings in the conquered lands. They also introduced the Latin language and Roman customs and otherwise "Romanized" defeated peoples, thus binding them to Rome.

The Brink of Destruction

In the decades following Rome's defeat of the Latins, the Republic was almost constantly involved in aggressive wars with its other neighbors. While fighting periodic battles with the Etruscans in the north, Roman armies moved into the Apennine foothills and clashed with the Sabines, Aequi, and Volsci. The Sabines fell to Rome by about 449 B.C., and the other tribes by the end of the century. The Romans then concentrated mainly on the struggle with the Etruscans. In 396 B.C., after a ten-year siege, Rome sacked the important Etruscan stronghold of Veii.

Rome now prepared for an all-out assault on the rest of Etruria. Before the Romans could launch the attack, however, they met with a sudden catastrophe that brought them to the brink of total destruction. At the beginning of the fourth century B.C. the Gauls, a warlike tribal people from central Europe, swept over the Alps into Italy.

As the Gauls neared Rome, the Roman consuls assembled a large army to stop them. The two forces met on July 18, 390 B.C., near the Allia River, a few miles north of Rome. When the naked, long-haired, and fearsome-looking Gallic warriors staged a wild, screaming charge, the mostly young Roman troops became terrified. They panicked, broke ranks, and suffered a major defeat. The triumphant Gauls then entered Rome and burned most of the city.

In the following months, despite their grim losses, the Roman people bravely rose to the challenge. They appointed a general named Camillus as dictator, and he quickly reorganized the troops and defeated the Gauls in a number of small skirmishes. The Gauls now agreed to withdraw to the north, providing the Romans paid them a large ransom in gold. The payment was made, and the invaders returned to the Po Valley.

Master of Italy

Though severely shaken and weakened by the Gallic onslaught, the hardy and resourceful Romans steadily recovered and resumed their campaigns of expansion. They rebuilt their city, surrounded it with a defensive wall, and created a new army that was more flexible and efficient. With this force, Rome conquered the Etruscans and others, including the formidable Samnites, in the century that followed. Over time, the Romans vigorously Romanized these peoples, absorbing them into the Roman state.

And year after year, Roman territory, military strength, and determination grew.

At last, the Greek cities of southern Italy remained the only barrier to Rome's complete mastery of Italy. Fearing a Roman attack, in 280 B.C. the Greeks asked Pyrrhus, ruler of the Greek kingdom of Epirus (in northwestern Greece), for aid. Leading a large army, Pyrrhus enjoyed some initial successes against the Romans. But he lost as many battles as he won. And after five years of indecisive fighting he abandoned the war and returned to Epirus. The Greek cities of Italy could not match the Romans militarily, and one by one they surrendered. By 265 B.C. Rome was the undisputed master of all Italy south of the Po River.

In two and a half centuries of nearly relentless wars, Rome had risen from an obscure farming town to one of the world's great military powers. The efficiency and stability of the Roman government and the Roman people's ability to endure hardships had contributed significantly to this success. So had Rome's prudent administration of conquered peoples. Although the Romans themselves recognized these strengths, they were convinced that destiny was the main reason for their success. The gods, they believed, had proclaimed Roman mastery over other peoples. The Romans would soon find their self-proclaimed superiority severely tested, however. Their attempt to expand their influence into the western Mediterranean, a region controlled by powerful Carthage, would plunge them into a struggle for survival far greater than any they had previously faced.

Chapter Three

Rome vs. Carthage: The Punic Wars

During the years that Rome was unifying Italy, the former Phoenician city of Carthage in North Africa had grown into an independent trading center and the most powerful city of the western Mediterranean. Carthaginian colonies and trading partners ringed the coasts of northern Africa, the islands of Corsica and Sardinia, and parts of Sicily. Carthage's large cargo and war fleets also controlled what is now southern France and eastern Spain. In the fourth century B.C. the Romans and Carthaginians had made a treaty agreeing to stay out of each other's sphere of influence. At that time the Romans were not a seafaring people and were preoccupied with their conquests in Italy. So they took little interest in the Carthaginians, and the two peoples rarely came into contact.

However, when the Romans became masters of Italy in the early part of the third century B.C., they were not content to halt their expansion. They sought to push outward from the Italian peninsula and control some of the territories dominated by Carthage. This caused rivalry, hostility, and eventually armed conflict between these two great powers. Rome and Carthage fought a series of bloody and costly conflicts that came to be known as the Punic Wars. (The term *Punic* comes from the Latin term meaning "Phoenician.") For both Rome and Carthage, the conflicts developed into bitter, all-out struggles for survival. They could end only in the total destruction of one combatant and the mastery of much of the Mediterranean world by the other.

Each Strong in a Different Way

In the early third century B.C. Rome and Carthage had much in common. Each ruled over a large territory inhabited by about 3 million people. Each had a legislative body that made laws and two chief administrators who ran the state. (The

A modern artist's reconstruction of ancient Carthage shows its circular harbor and ship sheds and the Byrsa hill rising beyond.

Carthaginian counterparts to the Roman consuls were called *suffetes*.)

Also, both nations had approximately equal military strength, although each was strong in a different way. The power of Rome's military lay in its large, highly efficient land army. In contrast, because they were primarily seafarers, the Carthaginians had little need for maintaining large standing armies. When Carthage required land troops, it hired mercenaries, foreign soldiers who fought for money. The nation's main power resided in its navies, consisting of the best ships manned by the most experienced sailors in the Mediterranean. They could strike quickly and with devastating force against both rival shipping and coastal towns across the western Mediterranean. As a result, Carthaginian vessels controlled the seas, allowing Carthage to maintain a tight monopoly on trade in the region.

Rome's Audacity and Secret Weapon

Constantly searching for ways to increase its wealth, Carthage was quick to take advantage of any situation that would expand its commercial influence and power. It found just such an opportunity in 264 B.C. Carthage captured the city of Messina, at the northeastern tip of the island of Sicily. This gave the Carthaginians control of the strategic Strait of Messina, lying between Sicily and Italy. The Romans were deeply disturbed, seeing Carthage's command of the strait as a threat to their security and prosperity. Claiming that the Carthaginians had violated the agreement to stay out of each other's respective spheres, Rome declared war.

Because Carthage controlled the seas and Rome had no war fleets, Carthage appeared to have a clear advantage as the First Punic War began. Carthaginian warships patrolled the eastern coasts of Sicily, bringing men, supplies, and weapons to Carthage's local strongholds. This prevented the Romans from successfully conquering the island.

But the ever practical Romans, seeing the need for a fleet of their own, quickly built more than 120 large warships. Less than five years after the war began, they launched these ships, which were outfitted with a new secret weapon called the *corvus*, or "raven." It was a long wooden gangway with a spike attached to the end. The raven stood in an upright position on

Why Rome Declared War

The immediate cause of the First Punic War was a dispute regarding control of the Strait of Messina (or Messana), the narrow waterway separating southwestern Italy from the northern edge of the island of Sicily. Rome needed access to the strait so that fleets of merchant ships could travel easily from Italy's western coasts to its southern and eastern coasts and vice versa. In the late 280s B.C. a band of brigands seized the town of Messina, situated on the western shore of the strait. Calling themselves the Mamertines, or "Sons of Mars," they killed most of the Messinian men, enslaved the women and children, and terrorized neighboring towns. Some of these towns were allies of the powerful Greek city of Syracuse, situated about 70 miles (113km) south of Messina. In 265 B.C. Syracuse's king, Heiro, led his army northward and besieged Messina. One faction of the Mamertines trapped in the city appealed to Carthage for help. The Carthaginians already controlled much of western Sicily. And they now saw a chance to extend their influence into the island's eastern sphere. Accordingly, a fleet of Carthaginian ships seized control of the strait, and captured Messina, a move that caused the Romans to declare war.

a Roman ship until the vessel was next to an enemy ship. When the Romans lowered the device onto the enemy's deck, the spike pierced the deck and held the gangway in place. Roman soldiers then poured across the raven onto the other ship. The building of the fleet, with its ingenious ravens, wrote the second-century-B.C. Greek historian Polybius,

> illustrates better than any other [example] the extraordinary spirit and audacity of the Romans. . . . It was not a question of having ade-

Roman soldiers leave their ship (at left), cross a corvus, *and engage the Carthaginians in hand-to-hand combat, at which the Romans excelled.*

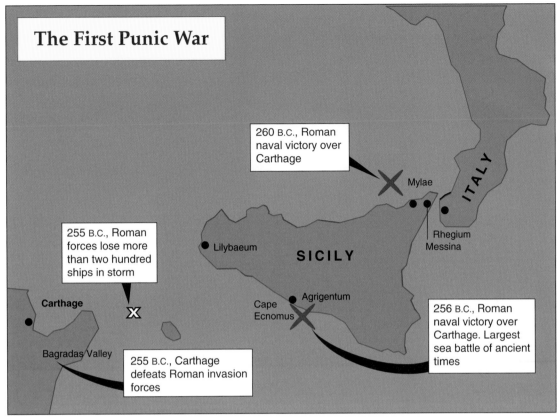

The First Punic War

260 B.C., Roman naval victory over Carthage

Mylae

ITALY

255 B.C., Roman forces lose more than two hundred ships in storm

Lilybaeum

SICILY

Rhegium
Messina

Carthage

Bagradas Valley

Cape Ecnomus

Agrigentum

256 B.C., Roman naval victory over Carthage. Largest sea battle of ancient times

255 B.C., Carthage defeats Roman invasion forces

quate resources for the enterprise, for they had in fact none whatsoever, nor had they ever given a thought to the sea before this. But once they had conceived the idea, they embarked on it so boldly, that without waiting to gain any experience in naval warfare they immediately engaged the Carthaginians.[8]

After winning several naval victories against Carthage between 260 and 256 B.C., Rome seemed on the verge of winning the war.

Horrendous Losses

However, Rome soon lost its advantage. In 256 B.C. it landed an army of just over fifteen thousand men, led by the consul Marcus Atilius Regulus, in North Africa. The Carthaginians raised a large mercenary army and hired a skilled Greek general named Xanthippus to lead it. The wily Xanthippus followed the Roman army at a distance as it plundered a number of Carthaginian villages. He waited until the Romans had completed a long march through an arid region and were thirsty and exhausted and then suddenly attacked. After hours of furious fighting, the Carthaginians were victorious. Many of the Romans were killed and a majority of the survivors, including Regulus, were taken prisoner.

During the next few years the Romans suffered other terrible disasters. One fleet

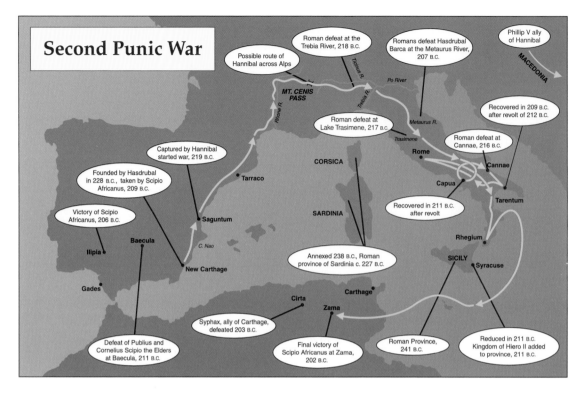

Possible route of Hannibal across Alps

Roman defeat at the Trebia River, 218 B.C.

Romans defeat Hasdrubal Barca at the Metaurus River, 207 B.C.

Phillip V ally of Hannibal

MACEDONIA

MT. CENIS PASS

Po River

Tiber R.

Rhone R.

Trebia R.

Metaurus R.

Recovered in 209 B.C. after revolt of 212 B.C.

Roman defeat at Lake Trasimene, 217 B.C.

Trasimene

Rome

Roman defeat at Cannae, 216 B.C.

Cannae

Captured by Hannibal started war, 219 B.C.

CORSICA

Founded by Hasdrubal in 228 B.C., taken by Scipio Africanus, 209 B.C.

Tarraco

Capua

Recovered in 211 B.C. after revolt

Tarentum

Victory of Scipio Africanus, 206 B.C.

Saguntum

SARDINIA

Baecula

C. Nao

Rhegium

Ilipia

SICILY

New Carthage

Annexed 238 B.C., Roman province of Sardinia c. 227 B.C.

Syracuse

Gades

Cirta

Carthage

Zama

Syphax, ally of Carthage, defeated 203 B.C.

Defeat of Publius and Cornelius Scipio the Elders at Baecula, 211 B.C.

Final victory of Scipio Africanus at Zama, 202 B.C.

Roman Province, 241 B.C.

Reduced in 211 B.C. Kingdom of Hiero II added to province, 211 B.C.

after another was destroyed in violent storms at sea, partly because the upright ravens made the vessels top-heavy and caused them to capsize. In all, Rome lost some six hundred warships and a thousand troop transports. It also lost more than 100,000 men to drowning—more than any other navy in a single war in history.

Moreover, the Carthaginians were able to inflict further defeats on the Romans. In 247 B.C. a brilliant war leader, Hamilcar Barca, took charge of Carthage's forces. For years he raided the coasts of Sicily and Italy, harassing and humiliating the Romans. Making matters worse, Rome spent such huge sums of money waging the long war that by 245 B.C. the city was nearly bankrupt.

Despite their horrendous losses, however, the Romans refused to admit defeat.

They courageously threw all of their remaining money, supplies, and manpower into building one last, large fleet. Commanded by the consul Gaius Lutatius Catulus, this fleet decisively defeated the Carthaginians off the coast of Sicily in 241 B.C. Surprised and devastated by this loss, Carthage sued for peace. The Romans demanded harsh terms, forcing their adversary to end its occupation of Sicily and to pay Rome heavy tribute (large sums of money) for the following ten years.

The Between-War Years

The victory over Carthage helped revitalize the war-weary Romans, providing them with a new burst of confidence in their own abilities. During the twenty years following the war, they renewed the policy of vigorous military expansion that had given them control of most of Italy. In a series of campaigns, Rome conquered Illyria, on the far side of the narrow Adriatic Sea. Roman armies also attacked and defeated the Gauls in the Po Valley, giving Rome control of most of extreme northern Italy.

Rome's economy also revived during these postwar decades. With Carthage defeated, Roman trade expanded around the Mediterranean and stimulated local Italian industries, such as shipbuilding, metalworking, and pottery making.

The Carthaginians, meanwhile, were not idle. While trying to rebuild his own nation's economy, Hamilcar strengthened Carthage's trading partnerships beginning

The Alps: A Dangerous Crossing

In September 218 B.C. Hannibal led about twenty-six thousand men, hundreds of horses, and thirty-seven elephants across the Alps in an endeavor that was as dangerous as it was audacious. In this passage from his history of Rome (excerpted in The War with Hannibal), *Livy described the difficulties the army encountered on reaching the highest point in the journey.*

There was a two-days' halt on the summit to rest the men after the exhausting climb. . . . The troops had indeed endured hardships enough, but there was worse to come. . . . As in most parts of the Alps, the descent on the Italian side . . . is correspondingly steeper, [so] the going was much more difficult than it had been during the ascent. The track was almost everywhere precipitous [steep], narrow, and slippery; it was impossible for a man to keep his feet; the least stumble meant a fall, and a fall a slide, so that there was indescribable confusion, men and beast stumbling and slipping on top of each other.

In addition to physical dangers, Hannibal's men had to fend off attacks by natives of the Alps.

Catastrophe at Cannae

Hannibal's victory over the Romans on a plain near the village of Cannae was the single worst battlefield disaster in Rome's long history. A huge Roman army of some seventy-five thousand or more troops, commanded by the consuls Paullus and Varro, confronted Hannibal's forty-five thousand troops on the plain. Anticipating that the enemy would attempt to overwhelm his own center, the Carthaginian set a trap. Instead of placing his strongest infantry in the center, he held these troops in reserve on the flanks and put his less formidable infantry units in the center. After the battle began, as expected, the Romans charged the Carthaginian center and easily pushed the enemy back. Meanwhile, the opposing cavalry units engaged, and the Carthaginian horsemen began to drive the Roman horsemen from the field. It was not long before Hannibal's giant death trap snapped shut on the unsuspecting Romans. The Roman infantrymen drove the Carthaginian center back so far that they passed by and between Hannibal's elite troops, still standing on the flanks. These fresh units now turned inward and attacked. At the same time, the Carthaginian cavalry, having chased away the Roman horsemen, wheeled around and assaulted the Romans from the rear. Surrounded, the Roman ranks crumbled.

in 237 B.C. This brought Carthage large quantities of silver, copper, iron, agricultural products, and fish. Hamilcar also intended to use Spain as a base of operations from which he could eventually renew war with Rome. Indeed, he hated Rome and imparted this hatred to his son, Hannibal.

Hannibal took charge of Carthaginian operations in Spain in 221 B.C. after the deaths of his father and Hamilcar's son-in-law. The young man turned out to be one of the greatest military leaders in history. Possessing a magnetic personality, strong personal discipline, and unmatched bravery, Hannibal inspired fierce loyalty in his troops. Livy later wrote:

Under his leadership, the men invariably showed to the best advantage both dash and confidence. Reckless in courting danger, he showed superb tactical ability once it was upon him. Indefatigable [untiring] both physically and mentally, he could endure with equal ease excessive heat or excessive cold. . . . Often he was seen lying in his cloak on the bare ground amongst the common soldiers. . . . Mounted or unmounted, he was unequalled as a fighting man, always the first to attack, [and] the last to leave the field.[9]

Continuing Carthaginian expansion in Spain, in 219 B.C. Hannibal boldly attacked

Saguntum, Rome's only ally in the region. The Romans interpreted this as proof that Carthage had been planning for years to reopen hostilities between the two nations. In 218 B.C. Rome sent ambassadors to Carthage with a stern ultimatum: Surrender Hannibal or face Rome's wrath. When the Carthaginians refused, the Romans declared war.

Hannibal's Bold Strategy

Hannibal swiftly enacted a daring strategy. Instead of fighting the Romans at sea or in Africa, as Carthage had done in the First Punic War, he decided to bring the conflict to Roman soil. His goal was to invade Italy and defeat Rome's armies. After this, he believed, most of the peoples recently conquered by Rome, including the Samnites and Gauls, would rebel and join him. In the fall of 218 B.C. Hannibal marched an army of twenty thousand infantry and six thousand cavalry northward from Spain, over the snow-covered Alps, and into the Po Valley. It had not occurred to the Romans that the enemy would make such a move because they viewed the Alps as a barrier no large army could ever hope to cross intact.

This element of surprise was exactly what the shrewd Hannibal had been counting on. And at first, his plan worked with brutal efficiency. The recently conquered Gauls were only too happy to cast off Roman rule and help the Carthaginians. Seeking to defeat Hannibal quickly and decisively, the Roman consuls Scipio and Longus attacked him near the Trebia River, several miles south of the Po River, in December 218 B.C. But the wily Hanni-

bal, expecting the assault, laid an ambush, and the Carthaginians destroyed more than two-thirds of the Roman army. A few months later Hannibal defeated another Roman army near Lake Trasimene, only 70 miles (113km) north of Rome. Nearly two entire Roman legions and their commanders were annihilated in the battle.

"When news of the disaster first arrived in Rome," Livy recalled, "terror and confusion swept the city. People thronged into the Forum . . . and began to call for the city magistrates. . . . No one knew what to hope for or what to dread."[10] In desperation, the Romans appointed a senator named Fabius Maximus as dictator. Fabius wisely refrained from risking his troops in battle with Hannibal. Instead, he followed Hannibal's army over the course of many months, harassing the enemy and making it hard for the Carthaginians to gather needed supplies. Meanwhile, Hannibal waited for the Italians to form a widespread revolt against Rome that never seemed to come.

Masters of the Western Mediterranean

In 216 B.C. when Fabius's term as dictator expired, the Romans elected new consuls. In the summer, these men led an army of more than seventy thousand troops to Cannae, in southeastern Italy, where Hannibal was camped with forty-five thousand Carthaginians and Gauls. On August 2 the armies faced each other on a flat plain near Cannae. And in one of the most brilliant displays of military tactics in history, the Carthaginian general delivered Rome a crushing defeat. At least fifty thousand

Above, Roman soldiers cripple Hannibal's war elephants at the battle of Zama; at right, a bust of Scipio, victor of the battle.

Romans died in the battle, including one of the consuls and some eighty senators.

When news of the disaster at Cannae reached Rome, fear gripped the city. Yet as they had done so often in the past, the Roman people, poised at the brink of ruin, met the crisis with courage, discipline, and dignity. They maintained a fighting spirit and refused to surrender.

In the meantime, Hannibal made the mistake of failing to follow up his great victory at Cannae with an attack on Rome itself. Instead, he continued to wait for Rome's subjects to rebel and join him. But few ever did. Eventually Rome carried the war to Africa, and in 204 B.C. Hannibal was forced to return to Africa to defend his native land. In 202 B.C., on the plain of Zama, southwest of Carthage, he was finally defeated by a skilled Roman commander, Publius Cornelius Scipio (later called "Africanus").

The second defeat of Carthage was Rome's greatest achievement to date. In the peace treaty signed in 201 B.C., the Carthaginians surrendered to Rome all but ten of their warships, Spain, and many other territories in the western Mediterranean. The Romans were now the undisputed masters of that huge region. At that moment, in the sea's eastern sector, growing numbers of Greeks worried that they might become Rome's next target. As it turned out, they had good reason to worry.

Chapter Four

The Mediterranean Becomes a Roman Lake

After defeating Carthage a second time, Rome became the dominant power in the western and central Mediterranean. Roman territory included Italy and the large islands of Sicily, Sardinia, and Corsica. Rome also controlled all of Spain and Illyria, which bordered Greece.

After many years of successful wars of expansion, many Romans favored maintaining an imperialistic foreign policy—using military threats and force to extend Rome's power and influence. A group of influential Roman politicians even advocated conquering Macedonia and the other Greek states clustered in the eastern Mediterranean. But a more conservative group, led by the senator Cato the Elder, was against expanding eastward. Cato argued that governing so many faraway lands would be too difficult and would waste Roman money and manpower.

As it turned out, in the first half of the second century B.C. Rome enacted what was essentially a compromise between these two positions. It conquered many of the Greek lands but at first did not impose direct rule on them. Instead, the Romans made them into vassal states, territories that could rule themselves as long as they supported and did the bidding of Rome.

For Rome, this period of rapidly shifting foreign affairs was also one of significant internal change. As the city's new empire grew, so did trade. Wealth from one end of the Mediterranean to the other flowed into Italy, stimulating the desire for luxuries most Romans were not accustomed to. The upper classes, into whose pockets most of this wealth flowed, enjoyed these luxuries and also used some of their money to support the arts, literature, and theater.

A well-to-do Roman family buys luxury items at a market in the era following Rome's conquest of the Greek lands.

Because only a few people had most of the money, the gap between rich and poor widened. Poor people seeking jobs or new lives flocked to Rome from all parts of Italy and the Mediterranean world, and the city became large and crowded. Many immigrants did not come willingly. During their conquest of Greece, for example, the Romans captured thousands of Greeks and forced them to work as slaves for well-to-do Roman families in Italy.

Wars in the East

Rome's conflicts with the Greeks began during the Second Punic War. While his armies were ravaging Italy, Hannibal requested help from King Philip V of Macedonia. At the time, Macedonia was one of three large Greek kingdoms ruled by the descendants of the Greek conqueror Alexander the Great. Alexander had defeated the Persians in the fourth century B.C. and created a vast empire stretching from Greece to India. But shortly after his death his generals had fought among themselves and divided up that empire. The Macedonian kingdom included most of northern Greece, some Aegean islands, and parts of Asia Minor. The Seleucid kingdom encompassed Syria and what is now Iraq. The Ptolemaic kingdom consisted of Egypt and parts of Palestine. These kingdoms frequently fought one another in costly and indecisive wars. But they feared the growing power of Rome more than they feared each other. Hoping to see the Carthaginians eliminate the Roman threat, Philip responded to Hannibal's plea for help by sending ships and supplies from Macedonia.

Once it had defeated Carthage, Rome sought revenge against Macedonia. In 200 B.C. the Romans attacked that kingdom, and in less than three years crushed its military. According to Livy:

Peace was then granted to Philip on the following terms: That all the [Macedonian] Greek cities, in Europe and Asia, should have their freedom and their own laws. . . . That Philip should surrender to the Romans the prisoners [he had captured], [and] all his decked ships, except five. . . . That he should have no more than 5,000 soldiers, and no [battle] elephants at all. That he should not wage war outside Macedonia without the [Roman] Senate's permission. [11]

Rome focused next on the Seleucid kingdom. In 192 B.C. the Seleucid king, Antiochus III, took over some of the Greek cities that had been freed after the war between Rome and Macedonia. Rome immediately sent troops into Greece and forced Antiochus to flee with his own soldiers to Asia Minor. The Romans gave chase and in 190 B.C. they decisively defeated Antiochus near Magnesia, in western Asia Minor.

The Circle of Popilius

This last victory did not end Rome's troubles with the Greeks, however. Philip V died in 179 B.C. and in the years that followed, his son, Perseus, who hated the Romans, began plotting with anti-Roman factions throughout the Greek sphere. Rome responded by sending more armies to Greece, and they demolished Perseus's

Greek Disunity Helps the Romans

One factor in Rome's favor during its campaigns in the east was the fact that the Greeks had long been disunited. During the Second Punic War, a prominent Greek orator—Agelaus of Aetolia—tried to warn his fellow Greeks about the dangers of disunity in a speech (excerpted here from Polybius's Histories*), but his plea went unheeded.*

It would be best of all if the Greeks never went to war with one another, if they could regard it as the greatest gift of the gods for them to speak with one voice, and could join hands like men who are crossing a river; in this way they could unite to repulse the incursions of the barbarians and to preserve themselves and their cities. . . . We should consult one another and remain on our guard, in view of the huge armies which have been mobilized, and vast scale of the war which is now being waged in the west. For it must already be obvious to all those who pay even the slightest attention to affairs of state that whether the Carthaginians defeat the Romans or the Romans the Carthaginians, the victors will by no means be satisfied with the sovereignty of Italy and Sicily, but will come here, and will advance both their forces and their ambitions beyond the bounds of justice.

forces in 168 B.C. at Pydna, in northern Greece. This time, the Romans completely dismantled Macedonia's monarchy.

In the meantime, another Seleucid ruler, Antiochus V, hoping to revitalize his kingdom and challenge Roman power in the east, invaded Egypt. Wasting no time, early in 167 B.C. the Roman Senate sent an ambassador named Gaius Popilius Laenas to Egypt with an ultimatum. When Antiochus greeted Popilius and went to shake hands, Polybius recalled, the Roman drew a circle in the dirt around the king. Popilius demanded that Antiochus withdraw his forces from Egypt and said that he must agree to do so before stepping out of

the circle. Fearing the same fate as Perseus and the other Greeks who had stood up to Rome, Antiochus complied.

The showdown in Egypt, thereafter referred to as "the circle of Popilius," became a symbol of Roman power and arrogance. For the next twenty years the Greeks did not dare challenge Rome's supremacy in the region. Then, in 146 B.C., two Greek cities, Sparta and Corinth, quarreled with each other, and Rome sent envoys to settle the dispute. Unhappy with the settlement, the Corinthians made the mistake of attacking the envoys. Rome responded swiftly and harshly. As a lesson to other Greeks, Roman soldiers attacked

The Romans Defeat Perseus at Pydna

Fought near Greece's northeastern coast in the summer of 168 B.C., the Battle of Pydna marked the climax of the third Macedonian war. The consul Lucius Aemilius Paullus led the Romans against a huge phalanx commanded by Macedonia's young king, Perseus. At first, the phalanx drove the Romans back. But soon the ground became uneven, hindering the Macedonian pikemen, and Paullus ordered small groups of his troops to move into some gaps that had formed in the Greek lines. Many Romans made it to the rear of the phalanx. Attacked from both front and rear, the formation rapidly fell apart. Perseus lost about twenty-five thousand men and soon afterward surrendered, while Paullus lost a mere one hundred men.

The Romans, commanded by Aemilius Paullus, defeat Perseus's phalanx at Pydna, spelling doom for Macedonia.

Corinth, massacred most of the inhabitants, enslaved the survivors, and burned the city to the ground. Despite Cato's warnings that imposing direct rule was a mistake, Rome did so, abolishing all democracies in Greece and making Macedonia a Roman province.

In only fifty-four years, Rome had reduced most of the Greek city-states and kingdoms to impotent, subservient Roman dependents. The last of the three large Greek kingdoms—Ptolemaic Egypt—was spared for the moment. But even though it remained independent, it was nearly as powerless as the others, and for the brief remainder of its existence it cowered in Rome's mighty shadow.

The Roman diplomat Popilius draws a circle around the Seleucid king Antiochus V, thereby using the threat of war to intimidate him.

Rich and Poor

As Rome conquered the Greeks and turned the entire Mediterranean into a Roman lake, all trade in that area came under Roman control. The money from increased trade, as well as from the gold, jewels, and other riches plundered from conquered peoples, made Rome more prosperous than ever. But with this prosperity came many problems. A small class of patricians and other well-to-do landowners and merchants became richer than ever, yet the majority of people remained poor.

Also, the number of poor grew steadily larger. One reason for this was that rich patrician farmers used their new wealth to buy large tracts of land and create huge estates called *latifundia*. Unable to compete, many small landowners gave up and migrated to the cities, especially Rome, in search of jobs.

As a result, Rome grew large, crowded, dirty, and noisy. The poor were packed into urban tenements, run-down apartment buildings with small rooms and poor sanitation. To meet the demand of the increasing population of urban poor, the owners of these buildings often added extra floors. But because they were so poorly constructed, the structures frequently collapsed, killing or maiming the inhabitants. The streets also became congested, sometimes unbearably so, a condition that would endure in Rome for centuries to come. Describing his daily ordeal in pedestrian traffic, the first-century-A.D. Roman writer Juvenal recalled in his *Satires:*

> We're blocked by the crowds ahead, while those behind us tread on our heels. Sharp elbows buffet my ribs, poles poke into me. One lout wings

Above, the ruins of the House of Diana, an apartment building, at Rome's port of Ostia; below, a modern reconstruction of the house and surrounding block in its prime.

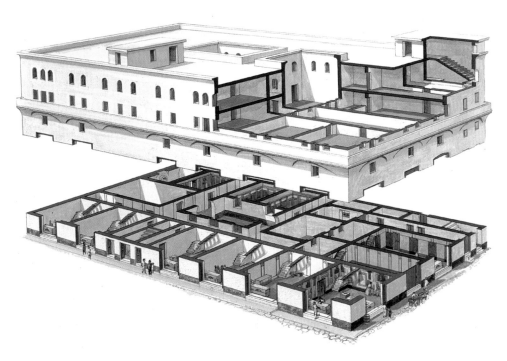

a cross-beam down on my skull. . . .
My legs are mud-encrusted, big feet
kick me [and] a hobnailed soldier's
boot lands squarely on my toe![12]

While tenement-filled slums sprang up
in some sections of Rome, elegant upper-
class houses were built in other areas. For
centuries, Roman houses, even those of the
well-to-do, had been relatively small, practical, and plainly decorated inside. But
during their conquests of the Greek lands,
the Romans saw and admired the large,
comfortable houses of wealthier Greeks.
Greatly influenced by Greek lifestyles,
upper-class Romans began enlarging and

adorning their own dwellings. It became
the fashion to fill a fine home with elaborate furniture, paintings, sculptures, and
other luxuries, many of them plundered
from Greek houses.

Women's Changing Status

Wealth also indirectly stimulated the
growth of women's rights in Rome. Believing that luxuries would spoil women and
make them disobey their husbands and
fathers, lawmakers had passed a special
law in the third century B.C. that forbade
women from wearing gold and beautiful
clothes and driving chariots. But in 195
B.C., after the first war with Macedonia,

Flexibility the Key to the Roman Army's Success

*A major reason the Romans were successful against the Greeks was that Rome's military sys-
tem proved superior to that of the Greeks. The latter utilized the phalanx, a large block of soldiers who stood in several ranks (lines), one behind the other. Carrying long pikes that pro-
jected from the formation, they marched forward as a unit. The Roman system, which allowed
smaller groups of men to act independently, was much more flexible, as Polybius pointed out
in this revealing passage from his history of Rome.*

The phalanx requires one type of ground only in order to produce its peculiar effect.
. . . Its use requires flat and level ground which is unencumbered by any obsta-
cles such as ditches, gullies, depressions, ridges, and water-courses, all of which are
sufficient to hinder . . . such a formation. . . . If the enemy refuses to come down [to
meet it on level ground] . . . what purpose can the phalanx serve? . . . [Also], the phalanx soldier cannot operate either in smaller units or singly, whereas the Roman formation is highly flexible. Every Roman soldier, once he is armed and goes into action,
can adapt himself equally well to any place or time and meet an attack from any quar-
ter. . . . Accordingly, since the effective use of the parts of the Roman army is so much
superior, their plans are much more likely to achieve success.

This modern reconstruction shows Rome's Capitoline hill (left) and main Forum (right foreground) as they appeared in the second century B.C.

thousands of middle-class and wealthy women crowded outside the Senate and boldly demanded the law be repealed. Fearing that this was the first step in a feminist drive for equality, Cato led the opposition to this change. "If each one of us," he declared,

> had set himself to retain the rights and the dignity of a husband over his own wife, we should have less trouble with women. . . . As things are, our liberty, overthrown in the home by female indiscipline, is now being crushed and trodden underfoot. . . . The very moment they [women]

begin to be your equals, they will be your superiors. Good heavens![13]

Despite the strong objections of Cato and other male traditionalists, however, the law was repealed. Moreover, other laws restricting women, both rich and poor, were struck down in the following decades. Although women did not gain political rights, they did win the rights to handle their own money and to sue their husbands for divorce.

Art and Literature

Household luxuries were only one of many cultural aspects that Rome borrowed from

based on Greek literary styles. The most popular writers of the day were the playwrights Terence and Plautus, who wrote mostly slapstick comedies based on well-known Greek plays. Another important writer of the age was the historian Polybius, a Greek who had been taken hostage during Rome's conquest of Greece and later became a Roman citizen. Polybius attempted to record the events, past and present, that had shaped the Mediterranean world he lived in. His largely unbiased and accurate history text remains an important eyewitness account of Roman life and events in this period. Meanwhile, his contemporary, senator Cato the Elder, wrote the first history of Rome in Latin. Cato also penned *On Agriculture,* a widely popular handbook on how to run a large estate efficiently.

Carthage Must Be Destroyed

Cato was even more famous for his oratory, particularly his speeches condemning Carthage. He and other conservatives believed that Rome had been too lenient on the Carthaginians at the end of the Second Punic War. Cato insisted that as long as Carthage existed it remained a dire threat to Rome. To emphasize his point, he ended every public speech, no matter what the subject, with the words "Carthage must be destroyed!"

Eventually, Cato's desire was fulfilled. Since its defeat in 201 B.C., Carthage had struggled to survive in the Mediterranean's Roman-dominated markets. Trying not to provoke the Romans, the Carthaginians had honored the treaty and refrained from

the Greeks. The Romans had long openly copied Greek art and architecture. But in the wake of the conquests of the Greek lands, Rome witnessed a new burst of interest in things Greek. Greek-style temples, theaters, and government buildings sprang up by the hundreds all over Italy. And Greek sculpture became so admired in Rome that many wealthy Romans became patrons of the arts. They supported hundreds of Roman artists who turned out copies of Greek originals for Roman homes, temples, and public buildings.

In addition, the Romans, who had produced no significant literature before this period, also began turning out writings

Cato shows his fellow senators some plump Carthaginian figs to remind them that Carthage had become too prosperous and must be destroyed.

making war on anyone. But in 149 B.C. the Numidians, another north African people, attacked Carthage, which had no choice but to defend itself.

Roman conservatives, spurred on by Cato, jumped at this chance to destroy their old enemy. Rome attacked Carthage once more, and Scipio Aemilianus, adopted grandson of Scipio Africanus, eventually captured the capital city. In 146 B.C., the same year that Rome destroyed Corinth, Scipio received an order to wipe Carthage from the face of the earth. The Romans killed most of the inhabitants, enslaved the others, and burned the city. Scipio and his friend Polybius stood on a hill and watched Carthage burn. The latter later wrote:

> When he had given the order for firing the town, [Scipio] immediately turned round and grasped me by the hand and said: "O Polybius, it is a grand thing. But, I know not how, I feel a terror and dread, lest some one should one day give the same order about my own native city."[14]

Thus, as one of the world's greatest cities vanished forever, Scipio correctly foretold that its destroyer, Rome, would someday meet a similar fate.

Chapter Five

The Struggle to Maintain Order

In the year 146 B.C. Rome's domain grew substantially. After the destruction of Corinth, all of Greece and parts of Asia Minor came under direct Roman rule. When Rome annihilated Carthage in the same year, northern Africa became a Roman province, too. Although Egypt and most Near Eastern lands were not yet provinces, they were largely Roman clients, weak states that ruled themselves but bowed to Rome in international affairs. All recognized that Rome was now the strongest military and political power in the western world.

But the Romans soon learned that administering such a large territory was no easy task. Their government had originally been designed to run a single city-state inhabited by one people. They found that this system did not work as well for a vast empire made up of many different peoples.

The result was that in the late second century and early first century B.C., Rome experienced both internal and external troubles as it struggled to maintain order in Italy and abroad. At home, the acquisition of new wealth began to have corruptive effects. Power struggles raged between the patricians and a class of well-to-do businessmen—the equestrians—as each sought to control the government. (The name *equestrians* came from *equites*, meaning knights, as in Rome's earliest centuries these men were horsemen in the army.)

Abroad, the main problem was the state of the military. On the positive side, the army was often effective because it was large and commanded by strong, talented generals. On the negative side, these generals came to wield too much power. Over time, Rome's armies became more loyal to individual generals than to the state. This inevitably led to bloody civil wars that threatened to destroy the republican system the Romans had worked so long and hard to build.

Increasing numbers of Roman peasants ended up working on the large estates of wealthy patricians and equestrians.

The Spread of Political Corruption

The troubles of the mightiest Romans during this pivotal period were most evident in Rome and its surrounding countryside. The patricians had monopolized political power for centuries, using their system of patronage to control the Senate. In the early second century B.C., wealthy patrician families had bought most of the land in the countryside to create the *latifundia*. So a small, elite, and conservative group controlled both the government and the land. Increasingly, however, this ruling class felt threatened by the growing influence of the equestrians.

One thing that these two classes had in common besides wealth and influence was their feeling of superiority to the common people. Nevertheless, both patricians and equestrians recognized that the support of the masses was essential to maintaining power and order. Therefore, all Roman leaders regularly appealed to the commoners to support their respective political positions and agendas. Because average citizens had the right to vote in the popular assembly, they often became political tools of the powerful. Elections became marred by open bribery and even violence as ambitious upper-class men used their money and social status to sway the results. The honesty and self-restraint displayed by earlier generations of Romans, both rich and poor, had begun to erode.

An Attempt to Restore Fairness

Some Romans admired these old ways and were disturbed by the corruption that increasingly riddled the system. They wanted to restore dignity and fairness to Rome by narrowing the huge gap between rich and poor. One of these concerned individuals was Tiberius Gracchus, a young man from a well-to-do family who was elected tribune in 133 B.C. Enthusiastic and well-meaning, he immediately proposed a new law that would restore all public land to the state. (Large tracts of public land had been leased to wealthy patricians, who were reaping big profits at the expense of poor farmers.) The government would then have to redistribute the land fairly among the people, both rich and poor, and limit the amount of land any one person could own. According to Tiberius's first-century-A.D. Greek biographer, Plutarch, the earnest tribune told audiences:

> The wild beasts that roam over Italy have their dens and holes to lurk in, but the men who fight and die for our country enjoy the common air and light and nothing else. It is their lot to wander with their wives and children, houseless and homeless, over the face of the earth. . . . The truth is that they fight and die to protect the wealth and luxury of others. They are called the masses of the world, but they do not possess a single clod of earth which is truly their own.[15]

The proposed law became controversial, and it was hotly debated in both the Senate and the streets. Fearing they would lose land and wealth if it passed, some patrician senators persuaded one of the tribunes to veto it. Because all the tribunes had to consent to any new legislation, the law was defeated.

With the aid of a loyal servant, Gaius Gracchus tries to take his own life as would-be assasins close in.

The tough, self-sufficient lower-level soldiers in Rome's emerging professional army became known as Marius's mules after the military reformer Gaius Marius.

Tiberius, however, was so determined to pass the law that he resorted to unconstitutional means. He quickly pushed a resolution through the popular assembly that threw out of office the tribune who had vetoed the land law. Tension gripped the city as some people sided with Tiberius and called him a patriot, while others denounced him as a traitor with no respect for Roman law. Capitalizing on the city's volatile mood, a group of conservative senators ran into the streets and stirred up a

The Rise of Marius

Born a pleb, Marius slowly rose through the military ranks to become a general and a consul. But he earned his stature as a national hero during a threat that arose in 105 B.C. The Cimbri and Teutones, large, restless Germanic tribes, had recently begun to overrun Rome's province in southern Gaul (now France). Two generals, one a consul for that year, fought the intruders near the Rhone River but were badly defeated. The Romans feared these "barbarians" would next march on Italy itself. So Marius, at the head of his army of "mules," marched northward to meet the threat, and in a tremendous struggle they decisively defeated the Teutones. About a year later, Marius inflicted an even more shattering defeat on the Cimbri near Ferrara, in northern Italy. These victories made him a hero of epic proportions, affording him the opportunity to amass unprecedented personal political power.

This bust is thought by some to be based on a portrait of Gaius Marius, one of Rome's most important military reformers.

riot against Tiberius. "The senators' followers were armed with clubs," Plutarch wrote. They "made straight for Tiberius, lashing out at . . . his protectors," who "were quickly scattered or clubbed down."[16] The tribune was killed, along with some three hundred of his supporters.

Ideas Ahead of Their Time

Many Romans assumed that Tiberius's reforms had died with him. Ten years later, however, in 123 B.C., his brother, Gaius Gracchus, became a tribune and also devoted himself to bringing about reform. Like his brother, Gaius proposed that many public lands be divided among the poorest citizens. Gaius also advocated other radical changes. For example, he suggested giving the same voting rights and citizenship privileges enjoyed in the city of Rome to all free adult males in Italy, no matter what their ethnic or tribal backgrounds. In addition, he called for lowering the price of corn so that more poor people could afford to buy it.

Because they were so controversial at the time, most of these reforms did not pass. Opposition to the citizenship law was especially strong. This was because most native Romans still held strong prejudices against people descended from ancient enemies like the Samnites and Gauls. Thus, on the day the law was to be voted on, opponents ignited violent street riots similar to those that had occurred a decade before. Gaius

The Social War Spurs Reform

Though Gaius Gracchus's call to give all men in Italy citizenship went unheeded during his lifetime, not long after his death this dream became a reality. The early first century B.C. witnessed growing unrest among Rome's Italian allies (various independent communities dominated by Rome). Though they had long contributed soldiers to Rome's armies, the allies were denied both a voice in Roman government and a share in the wealth gained by Roman conquests. The result was the Social War, which began in 90 B.C. Many towns in the southern half of Italy rebelled, and some banded together and established their own capital, which they called Italica. The surprised and outraged Senate sent several Roman commanders against the rebels in the following year. But they were unable to defeat them. By early 88 B.C., after much bitter fighting, the senators conceded the practical necessity of granting the former allies citizenship. A sweeping decree declared that all free adult males in Italy south of the Po Valley were hereby full Roman citizens. This move had the desired effect of inducing most of the rebels to lay down their arms.

died and his body was thrown into the Tiber.

The Gracchi had courageously but vainly attempted to restore fairness and order to the Roman political system. The problem was that their proposals were simply too far ahead of their time. But even though the brothers themselves had failed, the ideas they had championed lived on, and in time the Romans adopted many of the reforms. For instance, Rome granted citizenship to all free adult males in Italy south of the Po Valley in 88 B.C., just thirty-five years after Gaius's death. Eventually the Gracchi were remembered as Roman heroes.

Marius's Reforms

While Rome struggled with domestic affairs and reforms in the late second century B.C., it also encountered trouble governing its many diverse and often faraway provinces. One problem was that many of the provincial governors lacked the administrative skills to run the territories efficiently. Although some able governors were appointed, as a rule they served for only one year. Because they had to take so much time getting used to their posts, many aspects of provincial government fell into the hands of inexperienced native officials. Also, tax collection in most provinces was corrupt, and much of the money collected ended up in the pockets of tax collectors or local officials instead of paying for government services.

Another problem in governing the empire was raising enough well-trained troops to guard and police the provinces. Throughout most of the second century B.C., Rome had maintained its long-standing tradition of allowing only landowners to serve in the army. But as wealthy Romans bought up many of the small farms to create their large estates, the number of landowners decreased sharply. By the end of the century, therefore, it had become difficult to raise enough troops for the many garrisons needed in the provinces. Having a smaller army was clearly potentially dangerous for Rome. Conquered peoples sometimes rebelled and new enemies periodically threatened the realm's borders.

A popular general named Gaius Marius solved this problem after he became consul in 107 B.C. Marius eliminated the landownership qualification for military service and allowed any Roman citizen to serve. He also increased wages and gave all soldiers the same weapons and training, creating a new professional army much larger and more effective than the old one. "He gave his army an intensive course of training," Plutarch said.

> There was practice in running and in long marches. And every man was compelled to carry his own baggage and to prepare his own meals. This was the origin of the expression "one of Marius's mules," applied later to any soldier who was a glutton for work and obeyed orders cheerfully and without grumbling. [17]

Marius also significantly reorganized the army's structure. He reduced the basic organizational unit, called a century, from 100 to 80 men and created a new battlefield unit called a cohort. A cohort usually

consisted of 6 centuries, or 480 men. Each regiment, or legion, had 10 cohorts, for a total of about 4,800 men, although this number could vary somewhat under certain conditions.

In addition, military camp life became more organized and disciplined than ever before. A Roman marching camp was laid out in a large square featuring stockades and other stout defenses on the perimeter and a convenient grid of "streets," each lined by tents, on the inside. Polybius wrote:

> The arrangement both of the streets and the general plan gives it the appearance of a town. . . . Everyone knows exactly in which street and in which part of that street his tent will be situated, since every soldier invariably occupies the same position in the camp, and so the process of pitching camp is remarkably like the return of an army to its native city. When that happens, the troops leave their ranks at the city gate and each man makes straight for his home.[18]

As a result of Marius's reforms, the Roman army became the effective defensive and offensive tool that Rome needed to protect and enforce the rules of its empire.

A Few Ambitious Men

Although Marius had strengthened the army and the realm, he had also helped to create a problem that Rome had not previously encountered. Most of the soldiers were now volunteers and career men who looked forward to getting pensions or parcels of land when they retired. Because the state did not provide such allowances, to acquire them a soldier had to depend on

Cohorts Replace Maniples in Battle

Not long after cohorts were introduced in the late second century B.C., these battlefield units replaced the long standard maniples. Basic battlefield tactics, however, did not change very much. First, each cohort was, like a maniple, an individual unit that could act on its own. And on the battlefield, the cohorts typically formed three lines, just as the maniples had. A common arrangement of a legion's ten cohorts was four in the front line and three each in the second and third lines. One line of cohorts could advance on the enemy while the cohorts of the other lines waited in reserve. In fact, the cohorts were even more flexible than the maniples because they could more easily be arrayed in unusual formations. One that proved particularly effective was the "pig's head." It consisted of one cohort in front, two in the second row, three in the third row, and the other four in the fourth row, together creating a massive wedge that was highly effective in frontal attacks.

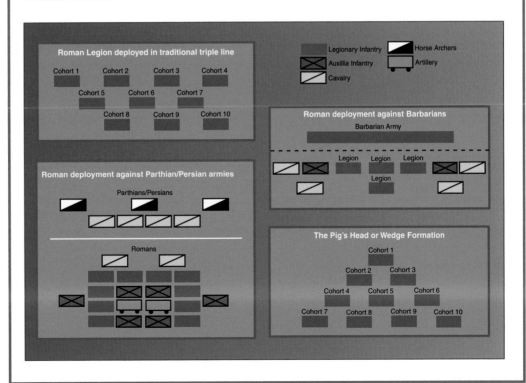

his general's personal generosity and influence with wealthy Romans. Over time, therefore, many of the troops became more loyal to their generals than to the government. This opened the way for ambitious, popular generals to use what amounted to their personal armies to oppose the state and even to march on Rome.

Marius himself became involved in the first such challenge to state power. For years he remained the most powerful and popular Roman general, but in 88 B.C. his former assistant, a general named Sulla, became consul and challenged his position. Both men won large groups of supporters in Rome. Marius, who had been born a commoner and worked his way up through the ranks, declared himself the champion of the plebs. In contrast, Sulla, an aristocrat by birth, gained the backing of the patricians and the Senate.

Shortly after becoming consul, Sulla left Rome to put down a rebellion in Asia Minor. With Sulla gone, Marius became the dominant force in Rome, and his followers murdered many of Sulla's supporters. Soon afterward, Marius died. But his supporters remained in power. Then, in 83 B.C., Sulla returned from the east and marched on Rome, becoming the first Roman general ever to attack the established government. A brief but bloody civil war ensued, after which Sulla appointed himself dictator.

Sulla's rule was harsh. He immediately murdered many of Marius's supporters and their families. "The city was filled with murder," Plutarch recalled, "and there was no counting the executions. . . . Husbands were slaughtered in the embraces of their wives, sons in the arms of their mothers." Sulla also ordered the killing of a number of wealthy people on trumped-up charges, confiscated their property, and then distributed it to his soldiers to keep their loyalty. According to Plutarch:

> Those who were killed because of some private hatred were as nothing compared to those who were butchered for the sake of their property. In fact, it became a regular thing to say among the executioners that "So-and-so was killed by his big mansion, so-and-so by his gardens, [and] so-and-so by his hot baths."[19]

Sulla retired and died in 78 B.C. And fortunately for Rome, the government rapidly returned to its normal structure and way of doing business. However, the civil war and Sulla's reign of terror had a lasting effect. These events had shown plainly that the Roman government was no longer strong enough to maintain order, whereas the army, in the hands of an ambitious man, clearly was. Rome now entered an era dominated by military strongmen. Under the pretext of providing order and stability, they would wield the power of empire and thereby threaten the very existence of the Republic.

Chapter Six

The Rise of the Military Strongmen

The power struggle between Marius and Sulla set a precedent in Rome. In the two decades following Sulla's death in 78 B.C., strong military leaders, some of whom were also wealthy aristocrats, repeatedly manipulated the government and the public to further their own careers. Foremost among the strongmen in this period were Pompey and Crassus. Both rose to power by saving the state from serious dangers, including pirates and rebellious slaves. For these ambitious men, however, their campaigns were less patriotic endeavors than they were opportunities to increase their personal prestige and power. In fact, Pompey and Crassus became rivals for the support of the people and control of the government. During these years only a few influential men openly opposed them and fought to maintain the integrity of the Senate and established government. Chief among these opponents was the noted senator and orator Cicero, who became a great champion of the faltering Republic.

Ascension of Pompey and Crassus

Gnaeus Pompeius, popularly known as Pompey, was among the first military leaders who attempted to fill the power vacuum left when Sulla died. One of Sulla's most trusted subordinates, Pompey won a number of battles against Marius's supporters during the civil war. Only in his mid-twenties at the time, Pompey earned a reputation as a daring and able soldier and became popular with Sulla's followers in the Senate and upper classes.

In 77 B.C. the Senate gave Pompey an important assignment. His job was to take an army to Spain and put down a rebellion led by a Roman general named Quintus Sertorius. A supporter of Marius, Sertorius had repeatedly defeated Sulla's forces in Spain between 80 and 78 B.C. In the following year, Sertorius had managed to take control of large sections of Spain and was still openly defying the Roman government. Pompey took forty thousand

Pompey, a skilled general, gained fame for his military exploits against pirates, escaped slaves, and rebellious generals.

troops to Spain and fought Sertorius for five years. Finally, in 72 B.C., the rogue general was assassinated by one of his own associates, Perpenna Vento, who then assumed command of the rebels. Pompey soundly defeated Perpenna and returned triumphant to Rome in 71 B.C.

While Pompey was acquiring glory in Spain, Marcus Licinius Crassus was rising to prominence back in Rome. Six years older than Pompey, Crassus was an aristocrat and the wealthiest man in Rome thanks to his ownership of silver mines and real estate. Like Pompey, he had been one of Sulla's loyal officers during the civil war. After Sulla's death, Crassus went back to managing his business affairs and waited for a situation to arise that would allow him to take command of an army.

Crassus's big chance came in 73 B.C. when a group of slaves at a gladiator school in Capua (about 100 miles [161 km] south of Rome) escaped and began terrorizing the surrounding countryside. They were led by a slave named Spartacus. Plutarch said of this remarkable man that he "not only had a great spirit and great physical strength, but was, much more than one would expect from his condition [i.e., that he was a 'lowly' slave], most intelligent and cultured."[20]

Under Spartacus's leadership, the escapees freed many other slaves in central Italy and built an army formidable enough to defeat several small Roman armies sent to destroy it. Eventually, the Senate dispatched forces led by the consuls. But Spartacus defeated them, too. Now fearful of mass slave uprisings across Italy, the government was desperate. Realizing that his rival, Pompey, was busy in Spain, Crassus offered to bring the rebellious slaves to justice.

One of Rome's Major Weaknesses

Crassus soon found that he had taken on a task far more difficult than he had anticipated. Tens of thousands of slaves had turned on their masters and joined the slave army. This force was growing daily and Spartacus and his fellow gladiators were training many of the recruits, mak-ing them more than a match for most Roman troops.

The fact that Spartacus's rebellion was so big and initially successful was a sign that the institution of slavery had become

Quintus Sertorius, a loyal supporter of Marius, is assassinated by some of his own men. The assassins soon met defeat at Pompey's hands.

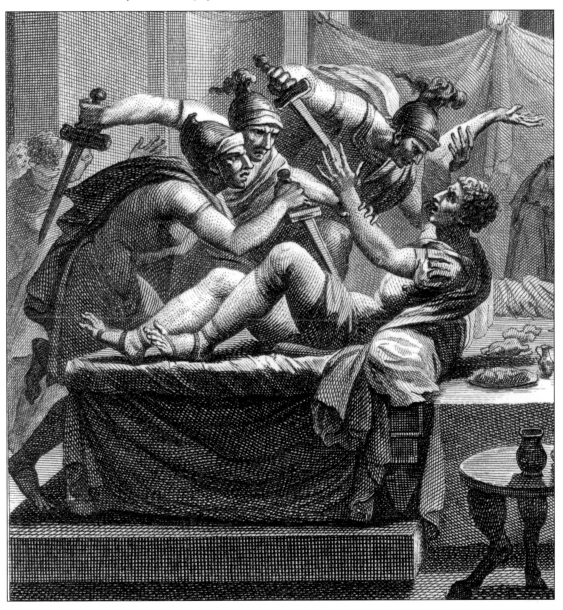

one of Rome's major weaknesses. The large number of discontented people living in servitude posed a constant threat to free Romans. At the time of the rebellion, perhaps a fifth or more of Italy's population consisted of slaves. In Rome itself, at least 200,000 of the city's 1 million inhabitants were enslaved.

Slavery had not always been so widespread in Rome. In the days of the kings and early Republic, most Romans were

Hoping to create a military reputation, Crassus eagerly accepted the job of defeating Spartacus and the slave army.

small farmers who did most of their work themselves. So there was little need for slaves. But over time the number of slaves steadily increased, especially during and after the third century B.C., when Rome began conquering foreign peoples. As was true across the ancient world, most slaves were war captives. Smaller numbers were bought in slave markets or born to people already in servitude.

Once a person had become a slave, he or she had no civil rights, and society viewed slaves as the lowest of the low. Even so, some slaves were well treated, particularly those who lived and worked in Roman homes. These slaves were referred to as *familia urbana*. In fact, some became trusted members of the family who were willing to die for their masters. However, just as many slaves were routinely beaten or otherwise ill-treated. Some were even killed by their masters.

With such a large proportion of Romans living in the misery of human bondage, slave rebellions were perhaps inevitable. The largest before that of Spartacus had occurred in Sicily in 131 B.C. A slave named Ennus had gathered some twenty thousand followers and set up his own mini-kingdom. It had taken a large Roman army two years to put down the uprising.

Crassus vs. Spartacus

Ennus's revolt was small, however, compared to the rebellion of Spartacus. By the time Crassus fielded an army against him in 72 B.C., the slave army had swelled to at least ninety thousand,

Spartacus Escapes

In his biography of Crassus (translated in Fall of the Roman Republic*), Plutarch provided these details about the escape of Spartacus and other slaves from a gladiator school.*

The rising of the gladiators and their devastation of Italy, which is generally known as the War of Spartacus, began as follows. A man called Lentulus Batiatus had an establishment for gladiators at Capua. Most of them were Gauls [from central Europe] and Thracians [from northern Greece]. They had done nothing wrong, but simply because of the cruelty of their owner were kept in close confinement until the time came for them to engage in combat. Two hundred of them planned to escape, but their plan was betrayed and only seventy-eight, who realized this, managed to act in time and get away, armed with choppers and spits which they seized from some cook-house. On the road they came across some wagons which were carrying arms for gladiators to another city, and they took these arms for their own use.

many of them well armed and well trained. Though Crassus recognized the danger involved, he also saw that he had a golden opportunity. If he could defeat Spartacus, he would be the greatest hero of the day and gain tremendous prestige and power. Indeed, he might well outshine Pompey.

Unfortunately for Crassus, his campaign got off to an embarrassing start. He ordered one of his officers, a man named Mummius, to take a small force and follow Spartacus's army until Crassus himself had positioned his main army to strike. Mummius had direct orders not to engage the enemy; however, perhaps out of arrogant contempt for "mere slaves," Mummius ignored his orders, attacked, and suffered a resounding defeat. Crassus then received more bad news. Pompey was winding up his Spanish campaign and would be returning to Italy to help fight the slaves. As Plutarch points out, Crassus knew "that the credit for the success would be likely to go not to himself but to the commander who appeared on the scene with reinforcements." Therefore, Crassus "made all haste he could to finish the war"[21] before Pompey arrived.

Crassus finally caught up with Spartacus late in 71 B.C. in the southern Italian province of Lucania. The two armies formed ranks and faced each other in an open field. Plutarch wrote that Spartacus called for his horse and

> drew his sword and killed it, saying that the enemy had plenty of good horses which would be his if he won, and, if he lost, he would not need a

This is one of numerous modern paintings depicting the death of Spartacus, whose rebellion severely tested the Senate and Roman army.

horse at all. Then he made straight for Crassus himself, charging forward through the press of weapons and wounded men.[22]

Most of the slaves, including Spartacus, were killed in the battle, although some escaped. Exactly as Crassus had been dreading, Pompey arrived just in time to track down the fugitives and thereby share in the victory. As an example to other slaves, the six thousand survivors of Spartacus's army were crucified along the road to Rome.

Pompey and the Pirates

The defeat of Spartacus brought Crassus and Pompey the complete allegiance of the army and great popularity with the public. The two men easily won election as consuls in 70 B.C. And in the decade that followed, they remained the most powerful and influential men in Rome. Each regularly sought whatever means he could to increase his popularity and military standing.

In these efforts Pompey was more successful as he executed one brilliant military campaign after another. His most famous exploits were against fleets of pirates, who for some time had been terrorizing the Mediterranean and interfering with trade. "The power of the pirates,"

Plutarch explained, "extended over the whole area of the Mediterranean sea. The result was that all navigation and all commerce were at a standstill." So in 67 B.C. the Senate sent Pompey to deal with the problem.

Pompey was to be given not only the supreme naval command but what amounted in fact to an absolute authority and uncontrolled power over everyone. The law provided that his command should extend over the sea as far as the pillars of Hercules [Strait of Gibraltar] and over all the

Large oared warships like this one were among those Pompey used to rid the sea of pirates. Not a single Roman ship was lost in the operation.

Cicero Exposes Catiline's Plot

When Cicero delivered his now famous first speech exposing Catiline's plot against the government, Catiline himself was present in the Senate chamber. Following is part of the dramatic opening of the speech (translated in Selected Political Speeches of Cicero*).*

In the name of heaven, Catilina, how long will you exploit our patience? Surely your insane activities cannot escape our retaliation forever! Are there to be no limits to this swaggering, ungovernable recklessness? . . . The patrols ranging the city, the terror that grips the population, the amassing of all loyal citizens on one single spot, this meeting of the Senate behind strongly fortified defenses, the expressions on the countenances of each man here—have none of these sights made the slightest impact on your heart? You must be well aware that your plot has been detected. Now that every single person in this place knows all about your conspiracy, you cannot fail to realize it is doomed. . . . What a scandalous commentary on our age and its standards! For the Senate knows all about these things. . . . And yet this man [Catiline] still lives! Lives? He walks right into the Senate. He joins in our national debates—watches and notes and marks down with his gaze each one of us he plots to assassinate.

In the Senate, Catiline sits alone (at lower right), shunned by the other senators, as Cicero (standing at left) denounces him.

mainland to the distance of fifty miles from the sea. . . . He divided the Mediterranean and the adjacent coasts into thirteen separate areas, each of which he entrusted to a commander with a fixed number of ships. This disposal of his forces throughout the sea enabled him to surround entire fleets of pirate ships, which he hunted down and brought into harbor.[23]

Incredibly, in only forty days Pompey swept the pirates from the seas, burning some thirteen hundred pirate vessels and capturing four hundred more, all without the loss of a single Roman ship. This feat made him a hero of epic proportions.

The Whims of Powerful Men

As great as Pompey's prestige and the power he and Crassus held was during these years, these men did not go completely unchallenged. In the 60s B.C. Marcus Tullius Cicero, the most brilliant lawyer and orator of the era, rose to prominence. He won the consular election, and soon became both a symbol and protector of old-style republican values, which seemed threatened by ambitious men like Crassus and Pompey.

Cicero's most dramatic accomplishment in this period was saving the government from a military takeover. Hearing that Lucius Sergius Catilina, popularly known as Catiline, a patrician and former colleague of Crassus's, was plotting to kill the consuls and seize the government, Cicero acted swiftly and boldly. In a series of powerful speeches, Cicero convinced the Senate to grant him and his fellow consul, Antonius, whatever powers necessary to foil the plot. Early in 62 B.C. Antonius attacked and defeated the small army Catiline was raising for his coup, killing the would-be usurper. Meanwhile, Cicero arrested Catiline's accomplices in Rome and ordered their immediate execution.

The rescue of the government made Cicero the man of the hour. But the reality was that he had defeated only a bungling, third-rate strongman. The two first-rate strongmen, Pompey and Crassus, were still as powerful as ever. Like many other Romans, Cicero became worried late in 62 B.C. when news came that Pompey, who had recently finished a military campaign in the east, was on his way back to Italy. The general fear was that Pompey would march his loyal and victorious army on Rome, as Sulla had. According to Plutarch:

> All sorts of rumors about [Pompey] were current in Rome. . . . It was thought that he would immediately lead his army against the city and make sure of absolute power for himself. Crassus secretly left Rome, taking his money and children with him.[24]

To everyone's surprise, however, Pompey did not make a major power play at this time. Instead, he disbanded his army and rode into Rome accompanied by only a few close friends. This was a shrewd move. By passing up a chance to become a permanent dictator, Pompey made himself more popular than ever with the common people. This, he may have reasoned, would give him the widespread support he would need if and when he was ready to seize power.

For a while it appeared that Pompey and Crassus would continue to be rivals for power in Rome. But by the late 60s B.C. another strongman—Gaius Julius Caesar—had gained prestige and influence nearly equal to their own. Caesar wanted to run in 60 B.C. for the consulship of the following year. Rather than vie with Pompey and Crassus for supporters, he chose the wiser course of convincing them to join forces with him. In a secret pact, later called the First Triumvirate ("rule of three"), the two older men agreed to help get Caesar elected consul. In exchange, Caesar would give them a say in running Rome after he was in power. What Pompey and Crassus did not foresee at the time was the degree of talent, ambition, and fortitude possessed by their fellow triumvir. In a meteoric rise to power that would make him a household name ever after, Caesar would soon sweep them aside and bring the Republic to its very knees.

Chapter Seven

Julius Caesar's Pivotal Exploits and Impact

The formation of a triumvirate by Caesar, Pompey, and Crassus was the strongest challenge yet to the integrity of the Roman Republic. Each of these men enjoyed varying amounts of control over or popularity with the army, the Senate, the wealthy classes, and the common people. By combining their considerable individual powers and influences, the three men were able to intimidate and overshadow nearly every governmental body and office.

But though impressive as a political force, the triumvirate was inherently unstable. Each triumvir was an ambitious, selfish man whose ultimate plans did not include sharing power with the other two. In time, the three-way alliance would shatter, igniting disruptive civil war and opening the way for one of the triumvirs to seize power as a single dictator.

Rule by Terror

After his election as consul for the year 59 B.C. Caesar immediately asserted the tri-

umvirate's hidden powers. He proposed a law that would distribute state-owned land among Pompey's veteran soldiers. When the tribunes, many senators, and the other consul, Bibulus, all opposed the law, the triumvirs used strong-arm tactics to get their way. Caesar's and Pompey's henchmen chased political opponents away from the Senate and other public buildings. They harassed Cato the Younger, the leader of the opposition, and so intimidated Bibulus that, out of fear, he remained in his house for most of his term as consul. Such use of force and terror ensured the passage of the land bill and other laws endorsed by the triumvirs.

Cicero was one of the few leaders of the old guard who was brave enough to speak out against the abuses. He argued that the Roman government had not been founded by and for a few individuals but was the result of generations of Romans working together for the common good. He blamed the current state of affairs on the

This bust of Cicero, the last great champion of the Republic, rests in a museum in Florence, Italy.

shortly after Caesar's term as consul ended in 58 B.C., Clodius managed to pass a resolution banning Cicero from Rome. The great orator reluctantly went into exile in Greece.

The Conquest of Gaul

Meanwhile, though Caesar was no longer consul, he and his fellow triumvirs continued to hold much power in Rome, a situation that would prevail for some time to come. For Caesar, however, political power was not enough. He still lacked the military experience and backing needed to compete with Pompey. So Caesar used his influence to get himself appointed proconsul, or governor, of the province of Cisalpine Gaul (the region consisting mainly of northern Italy). He also managed to get his hands on another province, Narbonensis (or Narbonese), lying beyond the Alps in what is now southern France.

When Caesar took charge of these provinces in 58 B.C., he found about twenty-four thousand troops at his disposal and immediately began raising more recruits. He required as large a force as possible. This was because his real interest was not in administering Narbonensis but in conquering the lands stretching westward and northward from it. The Romans saw this region, called Transalpine Gaul (which encompassed what is now most of France and Belgium), as vast, wild, and mysterious. Caesar described what little he knew of it in the famous opening lines of his *Commentary on the Gallic War,* the personal journal he kept of his campaigns:

steady decay of Roman values. And he called on all Roman leaders, especially the triumvirs, to recognize their duty to the state and to the people.

These words fell mainly on deaf ears, however, as Caesar and his powerful partners continued to intimidate the government. Moreover, they finally managed to muzzle Cicero. Caesar helped one of his associates, Clodius, to become tribune, and

The country of Gaul consists of three separate parts, one of which is inhabited by the Belgae, one by the Aquitani, and one by the people whom we call "Gauls" but who are known in their own language as "Celts." The three peoples differ from one another in language, customs and laws. . . . The toughest soldiers come from the Belgae. This is because they are farthest away from the culture and civilized way of life of the Roman province [Narbonensis].[25]

By conquering Gaul, Caesar hoped to gain a great deal. First, he would build a large, battle-hardened army loyal mainly to him. Second, he could use the riches plundered during the conquests to pay his henchmen in Rome and to bribe public officials to vote the way he wanted. That way, he could maintain his share of the triumviral power during his absence. Third, he would be defeating an ancient enemy— the Gauls—and expanding the realm, making him immensely popular with the Roman people as a whole.

Caesar accomplished all of these goals during the eight years he spent campaigning in Gaul. By 57 B.C. he had driven deep into northeastern Gaul and in the following year he subdued the tribes along the Atlantic coast. Many of the conquered Gauls rebelled in 52 B.C., but in a spectacular display of strategic skills and raw courage Caesar defeated them. By the end of 51 B.C. had subdued nearly all of Transalpine Gaul. He had fought more than thirty major battles, captured over eight hundred towns, and killed over a million people, an impressive or despicable record depending on one's point of view. Most Romans were clearly impressed because Caesar had added huge new territories to the realm. This greatly bolstered his political influence and popularity.

This is one of several surviving sculpted portraits of Julius Caesar, conqueror of Gaul.

"The Die Is Cast"

Also, Caesar now saw his chance to use this personal capital. By the end of his campaigns in Gaul, the triumvirate was falling apart. In 53 B.C. Crassus had died in a military campaign in the east, leaving Pompey the only triumvir in Rome. Rome and its government were in a state of turmoil and uncertainty. Though a skilled general, Pompey was a poor administrator and politician. He largely stood by and did nothing as rival factions in the government stirred up mobs and riots, and he allowed himself to become a tool of the conservative senators. These men sought to destroy the remainder of the triumvirate by pitting Pompey and Caesar against each other.

To this end, in January 49 B.C. the Senate declared Pompey a protector of the state. At the same time, the senators showed hostility to Caesar, whom they now greatly feared, and curtly ordered him to disband his army. When his associate Marcus Antonius (Mark Antony) objected, the senators drove him from the city.

Learning of these events, Caesar realized that he had a fateful decision to make. At the time, he and his troops were camped near the Rubicon River, then recognized as the boundary between his province of Cisalpine Gaul and Italy proper. If Caesar obeyed the Senate and disbanded his army, his military and political career would be

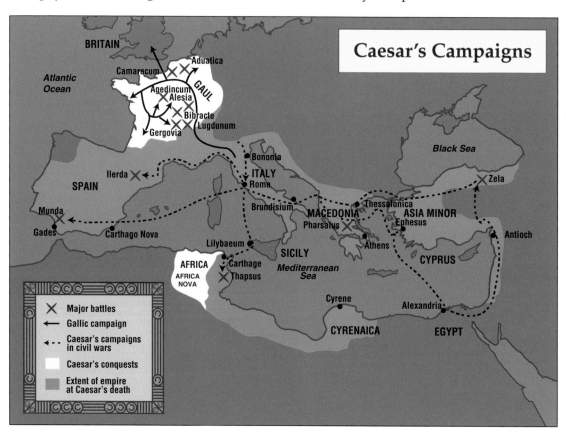

Caesar's Campaigns

X Major battles
← Gallic campaign
◄- - Caesar's campaigns in civil wars
▢ Caesar's conquests
▨ Extent of empire at Caesar's death

Setting an Example for His Men

During his Gallic campaigns, Caesar demonstrated that he was not only an excellent military strategist but a courageous and physically tough soldier who set an impressive example for his men. In his Lives of the Twelve Caesars, *the second-century Roman historian Suetonius recalled some of these qualities.*

Caesar was a most skillful swordsman and horseman and showed surprising powers of endurance. He always led his army, more often on foot than in the saddle, went bareheaded in sun and rain alike, and could travel for long distances at incredible speed . . . taking very little luggage. If he reached an unfordable river he would either swim or propel himself across it on an inflated skin; and often he arrived at his destination before the messengers whom he had sent ahead to announce his approach.

over. On the other hand, if he marched his men across the river, the Senate would see it as an armed attack on the state and order Pompey to retaliate.

Clearly, Caesar decided, he had much to lose by obeying the Senate and everything to gain by defying it. On January 10, 49 B.C., he told his officers: "We may still draw back, but once across that little bridge, we shall have to fight it out. . . . Let us . . . follow where [the gods] beckon, in vengeance on our double-dealing enemies. The die is cast."[26] With these words, Caesar led his men across the river, thereby plunging the Roman world into a devastating civil war.

Pompey's Demise

With Caesar approaching, many people in Rome and its environs panicked. Rome was "inundated as people came in from all the surrounding towns, escaping from their homes," Plutarch wrote.

The authority of the magistrates and the eloquence of orators were ineffective to exert control, and in this great stormy tempest the city nearly allowed itself to go under. On every side, violently opposed feelings were expressed in violent action. . . . Pompey's own state of mind was already sufficiently disturbed and it was made all the more confused by [the turmoil].[27]

Indeed, the widespread fear and confusion prevented Pompey from organizing a defense fast enough. So he, some of his troops, and many senators decided that their best bet was to flee Italy. Pompey traveled to Greece and immediately began raising an army to oppose Caesar. As for Caesar, he did not pursue Pompey right away. Instead, the conqueror of Gaul wisely took the time to consolidate his own power in Rome and to eliminate Pompey's supporters in Italy and Spain.

Finally, Caesar felt he was ready to confront his former triumviral partner. The pivotal battle took place on August 9, 48 B.C., at Pharsalus, in central Greece. Pompey commanded at least 40,000 infantry and 7,000 cavalry, while Caesar's forces numbered only about 22,000 infantry and 1,000 cavalry. Caesar made up for the enemy's superior numbers by deftly outmaneuvering his opponent on the battlefield. Realizing they were losing, many of Pompey's men retreated. Caesar's soldiers pursued them to their camp and beyond, while the humiliated Pompey, who had never before tasted defeat in his long and illustrious career, escaped to Greece's eastern coast. The enormity of Caesar's victory is reflected in the casualty figures. Pompey lost some 15,000 dead and 24,000 captured, while Caesar lost just 200 men.

Not long after his defeat, Pompey fled toward Egypt. The ruler there was a boy, Ptolemy XIII, a descendant of Alexander the Great's general of the same name. Pompey hoped that the Egyptians would give him refuge from Caesar. But Ptolemy's advisers warned him that helping Pompey might bring Caesar's wrath down on Egypt. So the young king ordered Pompey's murder. The second-century Romanized Greek historian Appian recalled:

A wretched little boat, with some of the king's attendants on board, was sent out to Pompey. . . . Sempronius, a Roman who was then serving in [Ptolemy's] army but had once served under Pompey . . . delivered greetings from the king to Pompey. . . . But when Pompey turned away he immediately struck the first blow and the others followed. . . . Pompey's head was cut off . . . and someone buried the rest of the body on the shore. [28]

The Ides of March

Ptolemy subsequently presented Pompey's head to Caesar, who arrived in Egypt a few days later. Despite having become Pompey's enemy, however, Caesar was shocked and dismayed at such brutal and disrespectful treatment of a high-placed Roman. Caesar decided to stay in Egypt for a while. And there he became embroiled in a power struggle between young Ptolemy and his older sister, Cleopatra. Caesar and Cleopatra formed an alliance and became lovers as well. Eventually, Caesar's forces defeated those of Ptolemy, who drowned while trying to escape, and Caesar restored Cleopatra to the throne.

Not long afterward, Caesar left Egypt and resumed his efforts against various opponents who still sought to defeat him. After a series of campaigns in North Africa and Spain, he returned to Rome in September 45 B.C. By this time, he had come to believe that the best way to achieve permanent peace and prosperity was to abandon

A nineteenth-century engraving depicts Pompey's murder, ordered by Egypt's young king and his advisors.

Death in the Senate

In his biography of Julius Caesar in Lives of the Twelve Caesars, *the Roman historian Suetonius described Caesar's death in the Senate on March 15, 44 B.C.*

As soon as Caesar took his seat the conspirators crowded around him as if to pay their respects. Tillius Cimber . . . came up close, pretending to ask a question. Caesar made a gesture of postponement, but Cimber caught hold of his shoulders. "This is violence!" Caesar cried, and . . . as he turned away, one of the Casca brothers with a sweep of his dagger stabbed him just below the throat. . . . Twenty-three dagger thrusts went home as he stood there. Caesar did not utter a sound after Casca's blow had drawn a groan from him; though some say that when he saw Marcus Brutus about to deliver the second blow, he reproached him in Greek with: "You, too, my child?" [Caesar had once had an affair with Brutus's mother and there were rumors that Brutus was Caesar's illegitimate son.] The entire Senate then dispersed in confusion, and Caesar was left lying dead for some time until three slave boys carried him home in a litter, with one arm hanging over the side.

Caesar is stabbed to death in the Senate. His killers mistakenly assumed that removing him would save the Republic.

many of the old republican ways and place most state power in the hands of a benevolent dictator. In February 44 B.C. he declared himself "perpetual dictator for the restoration of the commonwealth." This was a fancy way of saying dictator for life. In this way, Caesar began to transform the ailing Republic into what amounted to an absolute monarchy, except without the title of king. "Every kind of superhuman honor was devised and heaped on [Caesar] for his gratification," Appian wrote.

> Statues represented him . . . wearing a crown of oak leaves as the savior of his country . . . His person was to be sacred and inviolate [untouchable], he was to conduct business from a seat of ivory and gold, and . . . in honor of his birth they changed the name of the month Quintilis to Julius [July].[29]

These and other developments convinced some of the senators that Caesar was going to make himself king and dissolve the Republic. Believing they were acting as patriots, two senators, Marcus Brutus and Gaius Cassius, organized a conspiracy to assassinate him. They made their move on March 15, the so-called Ides of March, 44 B.C. Caesar visited the Senate that day, and soon after he entered the conspirators pulled knives from their togas and stabbed him to death. Ironically, his bleeding body collapsed at the base of a statue of his former rival, Pompey. The murderers, their clothes stained with blood, then ran into the streets crying "Liberty!" Their victory over Caesar proved a hollow one, however. The truth was that their beloved Republic was as mortally wounded as Caesar was. And the sounds of its final death knell would soon be ringing in their ears.

Chapter Eight

Octavian and the Collapse of the Republic

Julius Caesar's sudden death left a huge power vacuum in Rome. The senators who had murdered the dictator assumed that the Senate would quickly regain its traditional authority and prestige and undo the damage that Caesar and other ambitious men had done to the Republic. But this did not happen. Other powerful men quickly stepped in to fill the vacuum created by Caesar's elimination. Among them were two of Caesar's closer associates, Mark Antony and the military general Marcus Lepidus. Caesar had also left an heir—his teenage adopted son Gaius Octavius, popularly known as Octavian. The shifting intrigues, alliances, and power struggles among these three men and their opponents would keep Rome entangled in civil strife for another thirteen years. Eventually, one of them would emerge from the fray and restore order. But that order would be based on a very different governmental system than the one that had guided Rome for centuries.

The Rise of Octavian

After Caesar's death, Antony wasted no time in asserting his own authority. Some of this was legitimate and some probably less so. He was then serving as consul, which gave him a strong legal position in the government, but he also claimed certain extra powers that Caesar had allegedly allotted to his successor in some personal papers.

While some senators and others disputed the authenticity of these papers, Antony acted boldly by delivering an impassioned eulogy over Caesar's mutilated body. The members of the great crowd that had gathered were moved when Antony reminded them of all the good things Caesar had done for Rome. Then, Plutarch wrote,

> as soon as he saw that the people were deeply stirred by his speech, he changed his tone. . . . Picking up Caesar's robe, stiff with blood as it was, he unfolded it for all to see, pointing

out each gash where the daggers had stabbed through and the number of Caesar's wounds. At this, the audience lost all control of their emotions. Some shouted aloud to kill the murderers, others . . . seized burning brands and ran through the city to the murderers' houses to set them alight.[30]

Fearing for their lives, most of the conspirators fled the city.

It now appeared to many that Antony was all-powerful in Rome. But any expectations he may have had of taking Caesar's place were short-lived. Octavian soon arrived to collect his inheritance and Antony, who was handling Caesar's will, treated the young man in a condescending

Marcus Antonius (Mark Antony) reveals Caesar's mutilated body to a gathered crowd. Those who had murdered Caesar were forced to flee.

manner. This was a serious mistake, for Octavian was shrewd far beyond his years and just as ambitious as Antony. The young man began to negotiate in secret with Cicero and other senators who disliked and wanted to get rid of Antony.

Octavian also wisely backed himself up with some real military muscle. In October 44 B.C. he swiftly gathered a force of more than three thousand of Caesar's loyal veterans. In his own later synopsis of his deeds, the *Res gestae*, he declared matter-of-factly, "At the age of nineteen, on my own initiative and at my own expense, I raised an army by means of which I liberated the Republic, which was oppressed by the tyranny of a faction."[31] This "faction," of course, was Antony. The combined efforts of the Senate and Octavian soon drove Antony from Rome.

Cicero meets his untimely end at the hands of Antony's soldiers. The murder was part of a major political purge ordered by the triumvirs.

The Second Triumvirate

Octavian now demanded the consulship. The senators were reluctant, but the young man backed up his demand with the same troops he had used against Antony. In the meantime, Lepidus had joined forces with the deposed Antony. And as scholar Philip Matyszak aptly puts it, "Octavian made the cold-blooded decision that he would do better joining the other two than trying to defend the Republic against them."[32]

The result was another powerful alliance of convenience—the Second Triumvirate. In the winter of 43 B.C. the three men met in northern Italy and divided up Rome's lands and powers among themselves. They also agreed on a systematic campaign to murder their main rivals and enemies, including a number of senators. This move was also designed to fill the triumvirs' pockets with funds they needed to pay their armies. The plan was to confiscate the fortunes and valuable estates of the prominent and wealthy Romans they slew.

At the top of Antony's list of condemned men was Cicero, the leading symbol of the dying Republic. The great senator got wind of the danger and tried to escape. But Antony's henchmen caught up with him. They cut off his head and hands and nailed them to a platform in Rome's main square, after which Antony's wife, Fulvia, pierced the dead man's tongue with her dress pin.

Showdown at Philippi

The triumvirs' opponents were not all in Italy, however. After escaping to Greece following Caesar's death, Brutus and Cassius had been raising troops in hopes of reestab-lishing senatorial control of Rome. In the summer of 42 B.C., on the plain of Philippi, in northern Greece, their army faced off with that of Antony and Octavian. The soldiers on both sides, Appian wrote,

> were filled with a recklessness that was beyond the reach of fear. At the present moment they had not the slightest recollection that they were all Romans, and they issued threats against each other as though they were natural enemies by race. Thus their immediate fury overwhelmed their powers of reasoning . . . and both sides alike prophesied that that day and that battle would decided the entire fate of Rome. And decided it was.[33]

Indeed, after hours of fierce and bloody fighting, the triumvirs' forces won the day. Humiliated and distraught, Brutus and Cassius committed suicide, and the last chance of restoring the Republic died with them.

In the years that followed, an uneasy truce continued between the victors of Philippi. Antony and Octavian, who in time eliminated Lepidus by placing him under house arrest for the rest of his days, were content at first to maintain their alliance. During these years Antony took charge of Rome's eastern territories and clients, while Octavian maintained control of Italy and the western territories.

Cleopatra and Actium

A clash between the two most powerful men in the Roman realm seemed inevitable.

In fact, over time Antony and Octavian's truce disintegrated and the two men engaged in a propaganda war in which each tried to position himself to gain total power. Much of Octavian's smear campaign centered on Cleopatra, whom Caesar had restored to Egypt's throne in the early 40s B.C. In 41 B.C. Antony had summoned the queen to his headquarters at Tarsus (in southern Asia Minor). He needed money and supplies for an upcoming military campaign and hoped that she would provide him with both. The two became lovers as well as allies. And thereafter, Antony spent more and more time in Egypt. He also abandoned his second wife (Octavia, Octavian's sister) for Cleopatra, a move that shocked and disturbed many Romans.

Octavian took full advantage of Antony's situation. The propaganda machine in the capital claimed that Cleopatra was a scheming, power-hungry character who had bewitched Antony so that she could control Rome herself. Antony was portrayed at first as a dupe and a cad, and eventually as a traitor to his country. Though highly exaggerated, Octavian's propaganda was effective and swayed Roman public opinion heavily against Antony and Cleopatra. In the fall of 33 B.C. Octavian felt confident enough to declare war.

The new civil war consisted largely of a single battle. Because they controlled the east, the most populous sector of the realm, Antony and Cleopatra managed to gather large numbers of troops and ships. But they were slow in formulating a coherent strategy for the upcoming conflict. While the lovers wintered in southern Greece in 32–31 B.C., Octavian seized the initiative. Aided by a loyal associate and skilled military commander, Marcus Agrippa, he managed to trap Antony and Cleopatra in Greece.

In an effort to break out of the trap, the lovers met Agrippa and Octavian's forces in a large sea battle near Actium, in western Greece, on September 2, 31 B.C. In the words of the second-century Romanized Greek historian Dio Cassius:

> At the sound of the trumpet Antony's fleet began to move. . . . Octavian moved out . . . [and] suddenly made a signal and, advancing both his wings, rounded his line in the form of an enveloping crescent. His object was to encircle the enemy if possible or, if not, at least to break up their formation. Antony was alarmed by this outflanking and encircling maneuver, moved forward to meet it as best he could, and so unwillingly joined battle with Octavian. [34]

After a while, Dio said, the engagement came to resemble a land battle:

> Octavian's ships resembled cavalry, now launching a charge, and now retreating, since they could attack or draw off as they chose, while Antony's were like heavy infantry, warding off the enemy's efforts to ram them, but also striving to hold them with their grappling-hooks. [35]

Eventually, Cleopatra took her personal contingent of ships and fled the scene.

Cleopatra Makes a Spectacle of Herself

In his biography of Antony, Plutarch gave this description (translated in Makers of Rome*) of Cleopatra's grand entrance into the harbor at Tarsus to meet Antony.*

She came sailing up the river Cydnus in a barge with a stern of gold, its purple sails billowing in the wind, while her rowers caressed the water with oars of silver which dipped in time to the music of the flute, accompanied by pipes and lutes. Cleopatra herself reclined beneath a canopy of gold cloth, dressed as Venus [Roman goddess of love] . . . while on either side . . . stood boys costumed as Cupids, who cooled her with fans. Instead of a crew, her barge was lined with the most beautiful of her waiting-women attired as [minor goddesses], some at the rudders, other at the . . . sails, and all the while an indescribably rich perfume . . . was wafted from the vessel to the river-banks. Great multitudes [of local people] accompanied this royal progress, some of them following the queen on both sides of the river . . . while others hurried down from the city of Tarsus to gaze at the sight.

A seventeenth-century painting depicts Cleopatra's famous arrival in Tarsus. Soon, she and Antony became allies and lovers.

Previous page: A nineteenth-century woodcut captures the chaos and carnage of the huge naval battle at Actium.

She may have been trying to safeguard her and Antony's treasure, which she had aboard her vessels, so that they could continue to fund the war. Whatever her motives, Antony soon followed her in flight, leaving his troops behind to face the enemy. On reaching Egypt, the lovers found to their dismay that their power base

Father of His Country

According to Suetonius in his Lives of the Twelve Caesars, *after giving Octavian the name Augustus, the Roman senators and people bestowed on him the added honorific "Father of His Country."*

The first approach was made by the commons [members of the popular assembly], who sent a deputation [delegation] to him. . . . When he declined this honor a huge crowd met him outside the Theater with laurel wreaths [symbols of honor and glory], and repeated the request. Finally, the Senate followed suit . . . [and] chose Valerius Messala to speak for them all. . . . Messala's words were: "Caesar Augustus, I am instructed to wish you and your family good fortune and divine blessings; which amounts to wishing that our entire State will be fortunate and our country prosperous. The Senate agrees with the people of Rome in saluting you as Father of your Country." With tears in his eyes, Augustus answered—again I quote his exact words: "Fathers of the Senate, I have at last achieved my highest ambition. What more can I ask of the immortal gods than that they may permit me to enjoy your approval until my dying day?"

This idealized sculpted image of Augustus was found at Prima Porta, near Rome.

in the east had collapsed in the wake of their defeat at Actium. The following year (30 B.C.), soon after Octavian landed his forces in Egypt, they committed suicide.

From Octavian to Augustus

At the age of just thirty-two, Octavian had triumphed over all his adversaries and emerged as the most powerful figure in the Roman world. Like his adoptive father, Caesar, he believed that order could best be restored and maintained by the rule of a benevolent dictator. So in the months and years that followed, he gradually amassed for himself a wide array of powers that greatly transformed Rome's government.

On the surface, the new system resembled the old one in many ways. This was because Octavian wisely kept several of the traditional republican offices and institutions—the Senate, consuls, tribunes, and so forth. In reality, however, these were mere trappings, as he had the final say in all important matters. He held authority similar to both consuls and tribunes, for example, which meant that he could both propose and veto any law. He also exerted complete control of the army.

Thus, Octavian assumed dictatorial powers yet wisely avoided the formal titles of dictator and king, which he realized the Roman people had come to despise and distrust. Instead, he chose to project the image of a savior and protector of the people. In 27 B.C. the Senate, whose powers were now more ceremonial than real, bestowed on him the name Augustus, "the revered one." Octavian accepted this lofty title but also adopted the more modest one of *princeps*, meaning "first citizen." Whatever he chose to call himself, history came to see him for what he really was—the first in a long line of Roman emperors.

Augustus enjoyed a long, successful, and peaceful reign. After nearly a century of bloodshed, power struggles, and civil strife, the Roman people were actually thankful for the order and stability he brought them. In fact, over time most Romans came to remember the days of the Republic as a time of troubles, chaos, and uncertainty. And desires to restore the old ways steadily disappeared.

Although the system that had brought the Romans power and prestige for five hundred years was gone, Rome—in the form of the new Roman Empire—was still the most potent and influential force in the known world. The Romans were set to embark on a new journey of accomplishments, triumphs, trials, and tribulations. These would profoundly affect the many lands and peoples they would encounter and in numerous ways dictate the course of the next two thousand years of world history.

Notes

Introduction: A Genius for the Practical

1. W.G. Hardy, *The Greek and Roman World*. Westwood, MA: Paperbook, 1991, pp. 90–91.
2. Sallust, *Conspiracy of Catiline*, in *Sallust: The Jugurthine War/The Conspiracy of Catiline*, trans. S.A. Handford. New York: Penguin, 1988, p. 220. Sallust attributed this speech to the famous politician-soldier Julius Caesar, although the wording is more likely the historian's own.
3. Edith Hamilton, *The Roman Way to Western Civilization*. New York: W.W. Norton, 1993, p. 116.

Chapter One: Rome's Origins and Early Centuries

4. Livy, *The History of Rome from Its Foundation*, books 1–5 published as *Livy: The Early History of Rome*, trans. Aubrey de Sélincourt. New York: Penguin, 1960, p. 401.
5. Harold W. Johnston, *The Private Life of the Romans*. Stockton, CA: University of the Pacific Press, 2002, p. 31.

Chapter Two: Foundation and Expansion of the Republic

6. Livy, *Early History of Rome*, p. 141.
7. Quoted in Naphtali Lewis and Meyer Reinhold, eds., *Roman Civilization, Sourcebook I: The Republic*. New York: Harper and Row, 1966, p. 85.

Chapter Three: Rome vs. Carthage: The Punic Wars

8. Polybius, *The Histories*, published as *Polybius: The Rise of the Roman Empire*, trans. Ian Scott-Kilvert. New York: Penguin, 1979, p. 62.
9. Livy, *The History of Rome from Its Foundation*, books 21–30 published as *Livy: The War with Hannibal*, trans. Aubrey de Sélincourt. New York: Penguin, 1972, p. 26.
10. Livy, *The War with Hannibal*, pp. 101–102.

Chapter Four: The Mediterranean Becomes a Roman Lake

11. Livy, *The History of Rome from Its Foundation*, books 31–45 published as *Livy: Rome and the Mediterranean*, trans. Henry Bettenson. New York: Penguin, 1976, p. 124.
12. Juvenal, *Satires*, published as *The Sixteen Satires*, trans. Peter Green. New York: Penguin, 1974, pp. 95–96.
13. Quoted in Livy, *Rome and the Mediterranean*, pp. 142–43.
14. Polybius, *The Histories*, trans. Evelyn S. Schukburgh. London: Regnery, 1980, p. 530.

Chapter Five: The Struggle to Maintain Order

15. Plutarch, *Life of Tiberius Gracchus*, in *Makers of Rome: Nine Lives by Plutarch*, trans. Ian Scott-Kilvert. New York:

Penguin, 1965, p. 162.

16. Plutarch, *Tiberius Gracchus*, in *Makers of Rome*, pp. 171–72.

17. Plutarch, *Life of Marius*, in *Fall of the Roman Republic: Six Lives by Plutarch*, trans. Rex Warner. New York: Penguin, 1972, p. 25.

18. Polybius, *Histories,* Scott-Kilvert translation, p. 337.

19. Plutarch, *Life of Sulla*, in *Fall of the Roman Republic*, p. 105.

Chapter Six: The Rise of the Military Strongmen

20. Plutarch, *Life of Crassus*, in *Fall of the Roman Republic*, p. 122.

21. Plutarch, *Crassus*, in *Fall of the Roman Republic*, p. 126.

22. Plutarch, *Crassus*, in *Fall of the Roman Republic*, p. 127.

23. Plutarch, *Life of Pompey*, in *Fall of the Roman Republic*, p. 183.

24. Plutarch, *Pompey*, in *Fall of the Roman Republic*, p. 203.

Chapter Seven: Julius Caesar's Pivotal Exploits and Impact

25. Julius Caesar, *Commentary on the Gallic War*, in *War Commentaries of Caesar,* trans. Rex Warner. New York: New American Library, 1960, p. 11.

26. Quoted in Suetonius, *Lives of the Twelve Caesars*, published as *The Twelve Caesars,* trans. Robert Graves, rev. Michael Grant. New York: Penguin, 1979, p. 28.

27. Plutarch, *Life of Caesar*, in *Fall of the Roman Republic*, pp. 276–77.

28. Appian, *Roman History*, excerpted in *Appian: The Civil Wars*, trans. John Carter. New York: Penguin, 1996, p. 114.

29. Appian, *Civil Wars*, pp. 125–26.

Chapter Eight: Octavian and the Collapse of the Republic

30. Plutarch, *Life of Antony*, in *Makers of Rome*, p. 240.

31. Augustus (Octavian), *Res gestae*, in William G. Sinnegin, ed., *Sources in Western Civilization: Rome*. New York: Free Press, 1965, p. 104.

32. Philip Matyszak, *Chronicle of the Roman Republic*. New York: Thames and Hudson, 2003, p. 228.

33. Appian, *Civil Wars*, p. 272.

34. Dio Cassius, *Roman History: The Reign of Augustus*, trans. Ian Scott-Kilvert. New York: Penguin, 1987, pp. 57–58.

35. Dio Cassius, *Roman History*, p. 59.

For Further Reading

Books

Phil R. Cox and Annabel Spenceley, *Who Were the Romans?* New York: EDC, 1994. An impressive, well-illustrated introduction to the Romans, presented in a question-and-answer format and aimed at basic readers.

Fiona Forsyth, *Cicero: Defender of the Republic.* New York: Rosen, 2003. A well-written synopsis of the life and contributions of one of the greatest Roman senators—Marcus Tullius Cicero.

John Malam, *Secret Worlds: Gladiators.* London: Dorling Kindersley, 2002. A beautifully illustrated book that brings the exciting but bloody gladiatorial combats of ancient Rome to life.

Geraldine McCaughrean, *Roman Myths.* New York: Margaret McElderry, 2001. An extremely well-written introduction to Roman mythology for young people. The author's prose is enthusiastic and readable.

Don Nardo, *The Etruscans.* San Diego: Lucent, 2005. A detailed look at the rise and fall of these close neighbors of Rome, who had a profound effect on Roman history and culture.

———, *A Roman Senator.* San Diego: Lucent, 2004. Tells the story of the origins and workings of the Roman Senate and other republican institutions.

Richard Platt, *Julius Caesar: Great Dictator of Rome.* London: Dorling Kindersley, 2001. An excellent introduction to one of the greatest Roman figures, who was often at odds with and successfully weakened the Senate.

Web Sites

Ars Haruspicina (www.cs.utk.edu/~mclennan/OM/BA/Har.html). This site by John Opsopaus is a fascinating review of the Etruscan art and practice of divination, which the early Romans absorbed and performed.

Roman *Cursus Honorum* (www.vroma.org/~bmcmanus/romangvt.html). This site by Barbara F. McManus provides an excellent overview of the offices of the ancient Roman republican government.

Works Consulted

Major Works

Brian Caven, *The Punic Wars*. New York: Barnes and Noble, 1992. An excellent overview of these monumental conflicts, useful for scholars and ordinary readers alike.

T.J. Cornell, *The Beginnings of Rome: Italy and Rome from the Bronze Age to the Punic Wars (c.1000–264 B.C.)*. London: Routledge, 1995. A well-written, authoritative study of Rome's early centuries. Highly recommended.

F.R. Cowell, *Cicero and the Roman Republic*. Baltimore: Penguin, 1973. Though somewhat outdated, this remains a detailed, insightful analysis of the late Republic, its leaders, and the problems that led to its collapse.

Michael Crawford, *The Roman Republic*. Cambridge, MA: Harvard University Press, 1993. One of the best available overviews of the Republic, offering various insights into the nature of the political, cultural, and intellectual forces that shaped it.

Jean-Michel David, *The Roman Conquest of Italy*. Trans. Antonia Nevill. London: Blackwell, 1996. A commendable overview of Rome's early ambitions and wars.

Anthony Everitt, *Cicero: The Life and Times of Rome's Greatest Politician*. New York: Random House, 2001. A fine recent telling of the deeds, works, and influence of one of republican Rome's greatest senators.

Harriet I. Flower, ed., *The Cambridge Companion to the Roman Republic*. New York: Cambridge University Press, 2004. Highly informative, this is a collection of essays about the Republic by noted scholars.

Michael Grant, *Caesar*. London: M. Evans, 1992. A fine telling of Caesar's exploits and importance by one of the most prolific of classical historians.

———, *History of Rome*. London: Orion, 1996. Comprehensive, insightful, and well written, this is one of the best available general overviews of Roman civilization.

Erich S. Gruen, *Culture and National Identity in Republican Rome*. Ithaca, NY: Cornell University Press, 1995. An intriguing examination of early Roman culture and the mind-set of the Roman people.

———, *The Last Generation of the Roman Republic*. Berkeley and Los Angeles: University of California Press, 1995. A leading scholar covers the collapse of the Republic and makes the case that it was not inevitable.

Tom Holland, *The Last Years of the Roman Republic*. New York: Anchor, 2005. A very readable and informative new look at the Republic's demise.

Andrew Lintott, *The Constitution of the Roman Republic*. New York: Oxford University Press, 2003. Very well researched, this is a fine overview of the Republic's political offices and institutions.

Philip Matyszak, *Chronicle of the Roman Republic*. New York: Thames and Hudson, 2003. A useful overview of the Republic, with plenty of information about the leading figures and their interaction with the Senate.

Other Important Works

Primary Sources

Appian, *Roman History,* excerpted in *Appian: The Civil Wars.* Trans. John Carter. New York: Penguin, 1996.

Julius Caesar, *Commentary on the Gallic War,* in *War Commentaries of Caesar.* Trans. Rex Warner. New York: New American Library, 1960.

Cicero, *Selected Political Speeches of Cicero.* Trans. Michael Grant. Baltimore: Penguin, 1979; and *Cicero: The Republic and the Laws.* Trans. Niall Rudd. New York: Oxford University Press, 1998.

Dio Cassius, *Roman History: The Reign of Augustus.* Trans. Ian Scott-Kilvert. New York: Penguin, 1987.

Juvenal, *Satires,* published as *The Sixteen Satires.* Trans. Peter Green. New York: Penguin, 1974.

Naphtali Lewis and Meyer Reinhold, eds., *Roman Civilization, Sourcebook I: The Republic.* New York: Harper and Row, 1966.

Livy, *The History of Rome from Its Foundation,* books 1–5 published as *Livy: The Early History of Rome.* Trans. Aubrey de Sélincourt. New York: Penguin, 1960; books 21–30 published as *Livy: The War with Hannibal.* Trans. Aubrey de Sélincourt. New York: Penguin, 1972; books 31–45 published as *Livy: Rome and the Mediterranean.* Trans. Henry Bettenson. New York: Penguin, 1976.

Plutarch, *Parallel Lives,* excerpted in *Fall of the Roman Republic: Six Lives by Plutarch.* Trans. Rex Warner. New York: Penguin, 1972; and *Makers of Rome: Nine Lives by Plutarch.* Trans. Ian Scott-Kilvert. New York: Penguin, 1965.

Polybius, *The Histories.* Trans. Evelyn S. Schukburgh. London: Regnery, 1980; also published as *Polybius: The Rise of the Roman Empire.* Trans. Ian Scott-Kilvert. New York: Penguin, 1979.

Sallust, *Conspiracy of Catiline,* in *Sallust: The Jugurthine War/The Conspiracy of Catiline,* trans. S.A. Handford. New York: Penguin, 1988.

William G. Sinnegin, ed., *Sources in Western Civilization: Rome.* New York: Free Press, 1965.

Suetonius, *Lives of the Twelve Caesars,* published as *The Twelve Caesars.* Trans. Robert Graves. Rev. Michael Grant. New York: Penguin, 1979.

Modern Sources

Lesley Adkins and Roy A. Adkins, *Handbook to Life in Ancient Rome.* New York: Facts On File, 2004.

Ernst Badian, *Roman Imperialism in the Late Republic.* Ithaca, NY: Cornell University Press, 1968.

Mary Beard and Michael Crawford, *Rome in the Late Republic: Problems and Interpretations.* London: Duckworth, 1985.

John Boardman et al., *The Oxford History of the Roman World.* New York: Oxford University Press, 2001.

Peter Connolly, *Greece and Rome at War.* London: Green Hill, 1998.

Charles Freeman, *Egypt, Greece, and Rome: Civilizations of the Ancient Mediterranean.*

Oxford, England: Oxford University Press, 2004.

Michael Grant, *A Social History of Greece and Rome*. New York: Charles Scribner's Sons, 1992.

———, *The World of Rome*. London: Phoenix, 2000.

Edith Hamilton, *The Roman Way to Western Civilization*. New York: W.W. Norton, 1993.

W.G. Hardy, *The Greek and Roman World*. Westwood, MA: Paperbook, 1991.

R.R. Holloway, *The Archaeology of Early Rome and Latium*. New York: Routledge, 1994.

Ramon L. Jimenez, *Caesar Against Rome: The Great Roman Civil War*. London: Praeger, 2000.

Harold W. Johnston, *The Private Life of the Romans*. Stockton, CA: University of the Pacific Press, 2002.

Robert B. Kebric, *Roman People*. New York McGraw Hill, 2005.

Lawrence Keppie, *The Making of the Roman Army*. New York: Barnes and Noble, 1998.

J.F. Lazenby, *The First Punic War: A Military History*. Stanford, CA: Stanford University Press, 1996.

Chris Scarre, *Historical Atlas of Ancient Rome*. New York: Penguin, 1995.

Ronald Syme, *The Roman Revolution*. New York: Oxford University Press, 2002.

R.J. Talbert, *The Senate of Imperial Rome*. Princeton, NJ: Princeton University Press, 1987.

Thomas Wiedemann, *Greek and Roman Slavery*. London: Routledge, 1989.

Terence Wise, *Armies of the Carthaginian Wars, 265–146 B.C.* London: Osprey, 1996.

Index

plebeians, 27–29, 61, 66
Plutarch
    on Antony's eulogy for Caesar, 86–87
    on Cleopatra's entrance into harbor to
        meet Antony, 91
    on fear of Pompey, 75
    on Marius's military training methods,
        63
    on riot against Tiberius, 62
    on Spartacus's escape, 71
    on Spartacus's killing of his horse, 71–72
    on Spartacus's strength/intelligence, 68
    on Sulla's reign of terror, 66
    on Tiberius's proposed land distribu-
        tion, 59
    on town panic over Caesar's impending
        attack, 81
Polybius, 38–39, 49, 53, 55–56, 64
Pompey (Gnaeus Pompeius)
    army disbandment and, 75–76
    ascension of, 67–68
    demise of, 81–82
    First Triumvirate and, 76–77
    murder of, 82
    pirate defeat and, 72–73, 75
    as protector of Senate, 80
    Spartacus's defeat and, 72
Popilius (Gaius Popilius Laenas), 49
popular assembly
    commons and, 94
    elections and, 27
    lawmaking powers of, 29
    patronage system and, 28, 58
    Tiberius's land redistribution and, 61
Po River, 14, 34, 43
Poseidon, 22
pottery making, 41
Po Valley, 33, 41, 43, 62
praetors, 27
princeps (first citizen), 95
proconsul, 78
Ptolemaic Egypt, 50
Ptolemaic kingdom, 48
Ptolemy XIII, 82

Punicum, 23
Punic War(s), 35
    First, 37, 43
    Second, 48–49, 55
Pydna, 49–50
Pyrgi, 23
Pyrrhus, 34

quaestors, 27

racetracks, 13
Regulus, Marcus Atilius, 39
religion
    animism and, 18
    Greek concepts of, 22
Remus, 16–17
Res gestae (Octavian), 88
Rhone River, 61
roads, 13, 27, 33, 51
Roman conquests, 31, 33, 41
Roman Empire, 95
Roman Monarchy, 18, 22
Roman Republic
    Caesar's monarchy and, 85
    Cicero and, 67, 89
    establishment of, 24–26
    extinction of, 95
    First Triumvirate and, 77
    members of, 27
    Octavian and, 88–89
    slavery and, 70
    threats to, 57, 66, 72
    war involvement of, 30, 33
Romans
    conduct and, 27
    conservative lifestyle of, 22
    family importance and, 17–18, 22
    morals of, 27
    origins of, 14–15
    patriotism of, 30
    values of, 22, 24
Rome
    burning of, by Gauls, 33
    as city-state, 25

Picture Credits

Cover: Scala/Art Resource, N.Y.
akg-images, 83,
akg-images/Peter Connolly, 30, 31, 38, 41, 50, 52 (lower), 54-55, 60
akg-images/Rabatti Domingle, 71
akg-images/Southby's, 47
Art Archive, 11(lower left), 36, 61, 84
Art Resource, N.Y., 59
Bildarchiv Preussicher Kulturebesitz/ Art Resource, N.Y., 68
Erich Lessing/Art Resource, N.Y., 79
Scala/Art Resource, N.Y., 26, 27, 44 (inset), 64, 74, 78
Louvre, Paris, France/Bridgeman Art Library, 70

© Bettmann/CORBIS, 11 (upper left)
© Burstein Collection/CORBIS, 10 (right)
© David Lees/CORBIS, 23
© Charles and Josette Lenars/CORBIS, 10 (lower left), 14
© Araldo de Luca/CORBIS, 11(lower right), 16, 52 (upper), 94
Time-Life Pictures/Getty Images, 44
Mary Evans Picture Library, 24, 29, 51, 56, 58, 61, 69, 73, 88
North Wind Picture Archives, 72, 87, 92-93
Steve Zmina, 40, 68

About the Author

Classical historian Don Nardo has published many volumes about ancient Roman history and culture, including *The Punic Wars, The Age of Augustus, A Travel Guide to Ancient Rome, Life of a Roman Gladiator, Greek and Roman Science,* and Greenhaven Press's massive *Encyclopedia of Greek and Roman Mythology.* Mr. Nardo also writes screenplays and teleplays and composes music. He lives in Massachusetts with his wife, Christine.